MARITIME
PORTSMOUTH
A History and Guide

MARITIME
PORTSMOUTH
A History and Guide

PAUL BROWN

TEMPUS

First published 2005

Tempus Publishing Limited
The Mill, Brimscombe Port,
Stroud, Gloucestershire, w
www.tempus-publishing.com

British Library Cataloguing in Publication Data.
A catalogue record for this book is available from the British Library.

ISBN 0 7524 3537 X

Typesetting and origination by Tempus Publishing Limited
Printed in Great Britain

CONTENTS

AUTHOR BIOGRAPHY

Dr Paul Brown was brought up in Gosport and went to Gosport Grammar School. It was at this time that his interest in ships and nautical history developed. He left the area after graduating from Sheffield University and has since lived in Northamptonshire with his wife and two daughters. He is now a Senior Lecturer in Strategic Management at University College Northampton.

Back cover: The Mast Pond was excavated in 1665 and was used to store the mast timbers, which were left submerged to season for twenty to thirty years. In its present form it dates from the eighteenth century. It became a boat pond when the need for wooden masts ended. No.6 Boathouse (1846) at the far end of the pond is a fine brick and iron building which now contains an interactive exhibition about the modern Royal Navy. Although Victorian, No.7 Boathouse – the timber building on the left – provides a reminder of what the timber buildings of the dockyard were like before Georgian brick buildings replaced them. (Author)

INTRODUCTION

The maritime heritage of Portsmouth is described and celebrated in this book, which is timed to coincide with the bicentenary of the Battle of Trafalgar. For the past three hundred years the port has been the leading base of the Royal Navy, but its origins as a military harbour date back to Roman times when Portchester was first fortified. Since the time of Henry I expeditions have sailed from Portsmouth to wage naval and military campaigns in France, Spain, and much further afield. Henry VIII established a permanent naval dockyard there and from the Napoleonic era onwards Portsmouth was the Navy's most important dockyard and base. Portsmouth's history is thus inextricably entwined with the history of the Royal Navy and with some of the most momentous events in the history of the British Isles.

The naval heritage of Portsmouth is manifested in the fortifications, buildings, docks and preserved ships described in this book. At Portchester are the two thousand year old Roman walls, whilst the Round Tower in its present form dates from about 1494 – shortly before the building of the *Mary Rose*. Portsmouth vies with Chatham as the best preserved Georgian dockyard in the world. The original Georgian buildings survive and look much as they did in Nelson's time, though their functions have, in many cases, changed. Within this setting is found the most illustrious survivor from the sailing navy, HMS *Victory*. This combination of a fully restored ship-of-the-line in its contemporary naval dockyard is unparalleled and is the city's greatest attraction. The Victorian buildings which accompanied the Navy's transition from sail to steam are also mostly intact, and in good condition. As if that were not enough, all this is seen alongside the modern Royal Navy and its facilities – allowing fascinating comparisons to be made which illustrate the development of the Navy and its ships over three hundred years.

That this much has been preserved is something to be grateful for. Perhaps now though part of this heritage is also at risk. There are plans to convert many of the older buildings for residential and commercial use, no doubt a move welcomed by the Treasury. But this will alter the ambience of the historic parts of the dockyard and detract from

The launch of the battleship *Iron Duke* at No.5 slip in 1912. (Portsmouth City Libraries).

the authenticity of much of what has survived. From this standpoint the changes are unwelcome – it would far better to convert the redundant buildings into exhibition space (for related naval and maritime exhibits and museums) and even restore some of them to their original working facility so that they would become enhanced visitor attractions. There are lessons to be learnt from some developments of this sort which have increased the heritage and tourism appeal of Chatham Historic Dockyard.

On the positive side, however, the older parts of Portsmouth Dockyard are developed there should be an added benefit of access to parts of the yard that are currently prohibited areas or are only open on rare occasions such as the International Festival of the Sea. The tighter security introduced since the events of September 2001 has meant that only the immediate area between the Victory Gate (formerly known as the Main Gate) and HMS *Victory* is normally accessible, and the necessary relaxation of this, that development would bring, would be welcome.

Whilst the buildings have, by and large, survived, ships are ephemeral – often with only short operational lives. Most of the famous ships that have featured in Portsmouth's history have long since been broken up. Over the last twenty years or so there has been an awakening of interest in the preservation of the few historic ships that survive. As a result, at Portsmouth – in addition to the *Victory* – we can see an early Victorian battleship, a monitor from the First World War and the Royal Navy's first submarine. Unfortunately

Above: A close-up of the restored clock tower on the Middle Storehouse. (Author)

Right: HMS *Victory* afloat in Portsmouth Harbour in the early part of the twentieth century.

A fast catamaran ferry approaches the Round Tower. In the background is Spitsand Fort which was completed in 1878. It was one of four sea forts built to defend the anchorage at Spithead. (Author)

there is, as yet, no significant survivor from the Second World War at the port. The submarine *Alliance* comes close to this, but, although designed during the war, she was not completed until after the end of hostilities and was heavily modernized in the 1950s. The best surviving British warship from the Second World War is HMS *Belfast*, which is moored near Tower Bridge in London.

The attraction of Portsmouth's maritime heritage has been recognized and capitalized on at the very successful International Festivals of the Sea which have attracted crowds of a quarter of a million. The harbour also remains one of the country's busiest, thanks in part to the growth of the cross-Channel ferry activity. Meanwhile the Navy continues to contract, through both relentless 'salami-slicing' and the more drastic cuts of periodic Defence Reviews such as that in 2004. This adversely affects the economy of Portsmouth and slowly erodes the spectacle of the modern navy at Portsmouth. Yet we should welcome the fact that, by and large, such contraction has only possible because of the absence of major wars in the last fifty years. In 1946, the Navy had almost half a million personnel. In 1947 de-mobilisation had reduced this to 192,665. Now the overall strength of the Navy is 37,500 personnel and this will reduce to 36,000 over the next four years, with the seemingly disproportionate reduction in the fleet by three destroyers, three frigates, six mine countermeasures vessels and three submarines. It is probable that, for the first time in three hundred years the Royal Navy will be smaller than the French Navy. There is more than a hint of irony in the fact that this coincides with the Trafalgar bicentennial! The operational capability of the Royal Navy is now quite limited, meaning that there is

Boy seamen marching at HMS *St Vincent*, Gosport. (J&C McCutcheon Collection)

greater reliance than ever before on our defence alliances with other nations. Each war fought since the Second World War has been confined to a single theatre, was of fairly short duration, and (with the exception of the Falklands War) has been fought with the U.S. as the main alliance partner. Hopefully, these circumstances, and the absence of major wars, means that we will no longer have to send *all* of a generation to war: instead they can join us as we enjoy all that the maritime heritage of Portsmouth has to offer.

Paul Brown
March 2005

Boy seamen manning the mast at HMS *St Vincent*, Gosport. Formerly Forton Barracks, it became home to the boys' training establishment in 1927 and was closed in 1968. Only the main gate and the adjoining terrace remain, the rest of the site being a Sixth Form College. (J&C McCutcheon Collection)

THE FIRST DOCKYARD

Portsmouth Harbour is a natural sheltered harbour that has for many centuries provided a haven for the Navy and a port of embarkation for successive armies. It is complemented by the anchorage at Spithead which, like the harbour entrance, is shielded by the Isle of Wight from the prevailing south-west winds. These advantages have led to two thousand years of maritime activity there, and to Portsmouth's role as Britain's most important naval port during crucial periods in its history.

The Romans built a stronghold at Portchester in the third century as part of a chain of forts from Brancaster (in Norfolk) to Portchester. They kept ships there to repel Saxon raiders. Portchester was then known as Portus Adurni and, around AD 284, the Roman emperor Maximinian appointed a Count of the Saxon Shore to take charge of operations against the raids by the Teutonic tribes of the Saxons and Franks. This man, Caius Carausius, was a Belgian sailor and he became rich and powerful through captured booty and proclaimed himself Emperor of Britain. Maximinian and his brother Constantius, retaliated by sending a fleet to fight Carausius. Before they could land, Carausius was killed in York in AD 293 by a fellow commander, Allectus. Allectus then assembled a large fleet at Spithead, which sailed to intercept the fleet of Constantius. However, the two fleets passed each other in thick fog and no battle took place. Allectus was later killed by Roman soldiers but his men seized London. Part of the Roman fleet arrived on the Thames and quashed the rebellion, rounding up and butchering Allectus' men.

Portchester has the most complete Roman walls in Northern Europe. They are 20ft thick, and the front face contains bastions which accommodated ballista (Roman catapults). By AD 501 the Roman occupation had declined and a Danish Saxon named Port came with two ships to 'Portsmutha' and seized land from a noble Briton. Other raids and invasions by Danes and Teutonic Saxons followed in the ensuing centuries. Portchester was used by the Saxons, probably as a defence against Viking attacks, until some control was gained by the ships of King Alfred and his successors in the late ninth, and tenth centuries. However, Saxon kings were to rule England in the early eleventh

The Roman walls of Portchester Castle. (Author)

century and Harold sent his fleet to Spithead and the Solent in the summer of 1066, expecting an invasion by William of Normandy. After six months the fleet dispersed, many of the ships returning to London, and William landed at Pevensey.

Henry I built a castle within the Roman walls at Portchester and embarked from Portsmouth on several occasions for Normandy, as did his grandson, Henry II in 1174. After Henry II's death in 1189 his eldest surviving son, Richard the Lionheart, landed at Portsmouth as King of England. In 1194, King Richard I ordered the building of a dock in the area called the Pond of the Abbess, at the mouth of the first creek on the eastern side of the harbour, which was later to become the site of the Gunwharf. Here ships could anchor, and on the creek's mudflats they could be hauled out of the water for repair or cleaning. The dock was enclosed by order of Richard's brother, King John, in 1212 and Portsmouth became a principal naval port, superseding the Cinque Ports. It is believed that there were locks ('wet-docks' built near the high water mark, which were blocked with timber, brush, mud and clay walls at low tide) and a sea wall, and penthouses were built to store sails and ships' equipment. A fleet led by the King sailed early in 1214 for La Rochelle and Bordeaux in an unsuccessful attempt to regain lost territory in France. Around 1228, but not for the first time, the dock was badly damaged by storms and high spring tides, and was consequently abandoned. It had not been well sited and subsequent docks were to be built further up-harbour.

Despite the lack of enclosed docks, Portsmouth was used to prepare expeditions to France by Henry III, and in 1346 Edward III sailed from the port with a fleet for Normandy and victory at the battle of Crecy. In 1415, King Henry V assembled his fleet at

An artist's impression of the *Mary Rose* leaving Portsmouth in 1545. This illustration is influenced by design evidence from the recovered hull. (The Mary Rose Trust)

Portsmouth and Southampton and, embarking from Portchester Castle, sailed for France and the Battle of Agincourt. On his return, he ordered the building of the Round Tower, beginning the construction of the port's defences. He also purchased land to the north of the old docks for the construction of 'The King's Dock' but, following his death in 1422, it was not built and most of the King's ships were sold.

The next, and highly significant, event was the ordering in 1495 by King Henry VII of what is usually said to be the country's first dry dock. This was to be built on the land that Henry V had bought, in the area now occupied by No.1 Basin. It was built to accommodate the new *Sovereign* and *Regent* which were bigger than their predecessors. The timber-lined dock was first used by the *Sovereign* which entered in May 1496. Once in the dock, after gravity drainage at low tide, the entrance was sealed with wooden gates and clay, and the remaining water was then pumped out using horse-driven pumps. In 1497, the first ship was built at the new dockyard. She was the *Sweepstake,* of 80 tons, and was later renamed *Katherine Pomegranate* by Henry VIII in honour of Katherine of Aragon (the pomegranate was part of the coat of arms of the city of Granada). Shipbuilding temporarily became a more important part of the dockyard's work when Henry VIII succeeded to the throne, with the construction of the *Mary Rose* and *Peter Pomegranate* helping to establish a permanent navy. Henry VIII is often seen as the founder of the Royal Navy since he commissioned the first ships which had an offensive role rather than being primarily transports for the army. Thus the *Mary Rose* can be considered to be the first true English warship. The dockyard was expanded due to its strategic importance under the threat of French invasion and incursions such as that in 1545 when the *Mary*

Rose sank. During this period the Navy grew from having only twenty-one ships in 1517 to fifty-eight in 1546. Thereafter the dockyard went into relative decline, and the Navy contracted so that by 1578 there were only twenty-four ships – rising to thirty-four in 1588, the year of the Spanish Armada. Though small, the Elizabethan navy was very successful, and for the first the time came to national prominence through the exploits of Drake, Frobisher, Grenville, Hawkins, Howard and Raleigh. They used both the Queen's ships and privateers, but their forward anchorage was Plymouth. In 1623 Portsmouth's original dry dock was filled in.

Apart from the construction of one small ship in 1539 there had been no further shipbuilding at Portsmouth since the *Peter Pomegranate* in 1510. Shipbuilding resumed in 1649, under the Commonwealth, with the 4th Rate *Portsmouth* and thereafter became a more or less continuous activity for three hundred years. Portsmouth had been loyal to Parliament and prospered under the Commonwealth. Also, war had broken out with the Dutch and investment in the dockyards and the Navy was at a high level. The Navy grew rapidly to have 102 ships in 1652 when the first Dutch war started, and 173 ships in 1688. By 1656, when a new double dry dock was ordered, the yard at Portsmouth had a new ropery, a slipway, and a surrounding brick wall of over 400 yards length, as well as numerous workshops and storehouses. The dry dock was completed in 1658 but the dockyard's growth was slow compared with Chatham which, like Deptford and Woolwich, benefited during the Dutch Wars from its geographical position. During the final years of King Charles II's reign Portsmouth received a mast house (1685), and, under King James, a further drydock and twenty new storehouses were authorised. James' successor in 1688 was King William III who recognised the importance of sea power and was to initiate a high level of expenditure on the Navy and the development of the dockyards that is exemplified by the Historic Dockyard at Portsmouth.

THE HISTORIC DOCKYARD

In 1689 William embarked on war with France. Because of its Channel position Portsmouth experienced a period of renaissance and was second in importance to Chatham. A large ropery, mast pond, numerous stores and workshops, and dockyard officers' houses had been built. Two new wet docks and two dry docks were constructed on reclaimed marshland to the north of the existing yard. By 1698, when the wet dock which became known as the Great Basin in the nineteenth century was opened, Portsmouth had again become the most important dockyard, serving a Navy that had expanded rapidly during the eight years of war. By 1697 the fleet contained 323 ships, including 112 with fifty guns or more.

The Historic Dockyard that we see today includes, as its oldest buildings, a number built in the early eighteenth century, including the Porter's Lodge (1708), the adjacent Main Gate (now known as the Victory Gate) and Dockyard Wall (1711), the elegant Dockyard Officers' Houses in Long Row (1717) and the impressive Royal Naval Academy (1733). In 1717, new gates were fitted to the Great Basin (now known as No.1 Basin, adjacent to the dry dock now occupied by *Victory*). Two of the dry docks (Nos 5 and 6) in this area were built in 1698 and 1700 respectively and are the oldest remaining dry docks at Portsmouth. No.5 Dock and a similar one constructed at Plymouth were the first stone-sided dry docks in Britain, though the floor of each dock was still made of wooden planks positioned on piles. Previously dry docks had had timber sides, and the new stone construction gave greater strength and water-tightness as well as making it easier to shore up a vessel with timber baulks. No.6 Dock was originally constructed of wood but was rebuilt with stone sides in 1741. The other dry docks (Nos 1-4) adjoining the Great Basin had stone sides and masonry floors and were complete by 1803.

The early part of the eighteenth century saw battles with Franco-Spanish fleets during the War of Spanish Succession, and other wars with the French ensued culminating in the Seven Years War of 1756-63. A large navy was maintained – in 1756 there were 320 ships, including 142 ships-of-the-line (First to Fourth Rates). Following peace, expansion and development of the dockyard continued, with an ambitious plan which took in new ground to the north and south-east, and made extensions to docks and slipways. No.5 Dock, originally known as the Great Stone Dock, was altered in 1769 by moving it a little to the east so that the Great Basin could be extended. This allowed the basin to berth twelve ships-of-the-line for repairs afloat. When the Basin was enlarged, the original 1495 dry dock was uncovered. The other wet dock (the Upper Wet Dock) was converted into a vast reservoir into which the dry docks could drain, and from where water could be pumped. This reservoir still lies underneath the Block Mills. In 1770 the yard had a workforce of 2,155, compared to 1,080 in 1728.

The Great Ropehouse, some 1,030ft in length, was built in 1770. The upper floors were used for spinning of yarn and on the ground floor this was twisted into rope as the forming machine travelled the length of the laying floor. The spinning and forming were manual operations but steam assistance was introduced to ropemaking in the early nineteenth century. Also remaining are the Hatchelling House, the Hemp House and the Hemp Tarring House (all built in 1771). Hemp stored in the hemp house was taken for hatchelling – straightening and untangling the fibres by drawing them across rows of spikes on boards. It was then transferred to the spinning lofts via a covered bridge. Some of these buildings replaced those lost in two disastrous fires in 1760 and 1770. There was another fire in 1776, started by the arsonist Jack the Painter who was sympathetic to the American Independence cause. Because it was built of brick rather than wood, the new ropehouse survived but the interior had to be rebuilt. Jack the Painter was hanged on 60ft high gallows at the dockyard gate and his remains were suspended in chains at Fort Blockhouse for several years as a warning to others. With the advent of the steam navy demand for rope reduced and the ropery ceased production in 1868: the buildings were then used as storehouses. So effectively had the ropery split the dockyard in two that the opportunity was taken to drive an archway through it.

Other buildings still surviving from this period include the three Great Storehouses (1763, 1776 and 1782), which can be seen on the left of the road between the Victory Gate and HMS *Victory*. Originally they stood on the water's edge and there was a jetty on the harbour side of the buildings allowing boats to come and collect gear and stores, often for transfer to ships lying at Spithead since sailing ships would usually avoid the tricky business of getting in and out of the harbour unless they were going into dock for repairs. The rudimentary jetty became part of the Camber (1785) which was built of stone (not to be confused with the commercial Camber in Old Portsmouth). This small inner harbour can be seen near the Semaphore Tower, behind the South Railway Jetty. The original Georgian Semaphore Tower was destroyed by fire in 1913 but was rebuilt in a similar style, as office accommodation, in the 1920s. One of the original dockyard gates, Lion Gate, dating from 1777, was relocated to form the arch below the Tower. The clockhouse on the Middle Storehouse was installed in 1992, replacing the original which had been destroyed by German incendiary bombs during the 1941 blitz on Portsmouth. Storehouse No.11, the oldest and most northerly of the three, now houses the Royal Naval Museum including the Sailing Navy Gallery and the Nelson Exhibition.

Built around the same time as the Great Storehouses, and opposite them, running parallel with the Great Ropery, are three more storehouses – the East Sea Store, and the West and East Hemp Houses.

The preserved monitor *M33* seen in No.1 Dock, a dry dock that was opened in 1801. Prominent are the stone aulters or steps which are divided by chutes for sliding materials to the bottom. In the background, at Pitch House Jetty, is HMS *Ark Royal*. (Author)

Another group of four Georgian storehouses was constructed to the east of the Great Basin around 1782 of which three survive – the twin South-East and South-West Buildings and the North-West Building. The South-East (now No.25 Store) is architecturally the most attractive, having been altered less than the other two.

The Royal Naval Academy (1733) was a college for naval officers with accommodation for a professor, a governor and forty young gentlemen aged 13-16, who were the sons of noblemen and gentlemen. The original curriculum included French, drawing, fencing and the use of the firelock, plus Latin from 1749 onwards. However, the college was not welcomed by naval officers because it undermined their own privilege of patronage in appointing boys to their ships. The education given at the college was poor and the scholars gained a reputation for swearing, drunkenness and idleness. In 1766, an enquiry by the Port Admiral led to the dismissal of the headmaster, mathematics tutor and a number of scholars. In 1773 there were a series of reforms, and the admission rules were altered to allow boys as young as eleven, who were sons of naval officers, to be accepted. By then the curriculum included writing, mathematics, navigation, gunnery, fortifications, dancing and the use of the firelock. Scholars could stay for up to five years – but problems with their behaviour persisted. They stayed out all night drinking at 'bawdy houses' and their heads 'abounded in vermin'. In the summer they went to Grange, near Gosport, to fight with the gypsies who camped there. They had instructions 'not to throw stones over

The Great Storehouses were imposing symbols of the rapidly expanding Navy, meeting demands from the fleet which grew from 272 ships in 1702 to 949 ships in 1805. Seen here are the Middle (No.10) and North (No.11) Storehouses. Each has three floors, an attic and a cellar, and the inner walls are faced with timber. The North Store houses the Royal Naval Museum. (Author)

the wall, or go to a billiard table'. In 1801 Lord St Vincent wrote 'The Royal Academy at Portsmouth, which is a sink of vice and abomination, should be abolished....' It was not abolished but was reconstituted in 1806, renamed the Royal Naval College, and finally gained some respect and credibility. In 1874-75 the activity was transferred to Greenwich and later Dartmouth. The building continued to be used for officer training, and from 1906 to 1941 was the Royal Naval School of Navigation (HMS *Dryad*). It is now an officers' mess.

Admiralty House (1787) also survives and was the grandest of the Royal Dockyard commissioner's houses on account of the frequent visits to it of King George III. The King had reviewed the fleet at Spithead in 1773 and 1778, and in 1794 he went aboard the flagship *Queen Charlotte* at Spithead after Howe's victory over the French on the Glorious First of June.

Building ships for the sailing Navy remained an important activity at Portmouth throughout the eighteenth and the first half of the nineteenth century. Between 1750 and 1840 twenty-six Ships-of-the-Line (First, Second and Third Rates) were built, as well as over eighty smaller vessels. The largest Ship-of the-Line built at Portsmouth was the 110-gun *Queen* of 1839, but even she was a little smaller than the Chatham-built *Victory*. The ship had been laid down as the *Royal Frederick* but was renamed before her launch, in honour of the new Queen. In 1842 Queen Victoria went aboard the *Queen* at Spithead during her first visit to Portsmouth after accession. She had arrived at Portsmouth by

The Porter's Lodge (1708) is the oldest remaining building in the dockyard. The Porter guarded the boundaries, prevented theft by dockyard workers, and rang the muster bell, closing the gate against latecomers. He also sold beer to the workers. (Author)

coach and four and stayed at Admiralty House. Accompanying her were Prince Albert and the aged Duke of Wellington.

Technological change came to the dockyard in 1797 when a small steam engine was installed to replace a horse-powered pump which emptied the Great Stone Dock's sump into the reservoir and also powered the sawmills. This was the first use of steam power in a Royal Dockyard and was soon followed by the design of Marc Isambard Brunel (father of Isambard Kingdom Brunel) for a steam-powered, block-making machine. These were the first powered mass production machines and were installed in the Block Mills between 1802 and 1806. Blocks were simple wooden-enclosed pulleys used extensively on sailing ships. The building can be seen on the north side of the Great Basin. The new equipment allowed 110 skilled blockmakers to be replaced by only ten machinists. Examples of the original machines can be seen at the Science Museum in London and at the Dockyard Apprentice exhibition in No.7 Boathouse at Portsmouth. Despite these innovations the dockyard labour force continued to increase during the Napoleonic wars, reaching 3,900 by 1814. At this time the dockyard was the world's largest industrial complex.

In 1832, a boiler shop was opened in the yard for the repair of both stationary and marine boilers and, in 1835, the first steam-driven warship to be built at Portsmouth was launched. She was the *Hermes*, a 6-gun paddle sloop. Portsmouth was the last of the home dockyards to start building steam warships and would require new facilities to meet the emerging needs of marine engineering and iron ship repair and construction.

Left: The Porter's Garden has been restored using the principles of eighteenth-century garden design. To see this garden you should turn right immediately beyond the Porter's Lodge after entering the Victory Gate. (Author)

Below: The interior of the Block Mills, photographed in 1910. The steam-powered mills were said to be the world's first use of machine tools for mass production. A 74-gun ship required some 1,400 pulley blocks for the running gear of the sails and for handling the guns. Annual production peaked at 140,000 blocks during the Crimean War. As the Navy changed from sail to steam the demand for blocks declined rapidly, but they continued to be produced on a limited scale until the 1960s when the Block Mills were closed. (Portsmouth City Museums)

Above: The Royal Naval Academy, which opened in 1733. (Author)

Below: Number One Basin with the First World War monitor *M33* in the foreground and the minehunter HMS *Bridport* alongside the basin wall. (Author)

The Block Mills (centre) and Wood and Metal Mills (right and left respectively) buildings. In the foreground is No.6 Dock. (Author)

Marc Isambard Brunel, a farmer's son, was born in 1769 in the hamlet of Hacqueville in northern France, and served in the French Navy for six years. As a royalist, he had to flee during the French Revolution to the United States, where he spent several years as an architect and engineer. He came to England in 1799 to show his method for making ships' blocks by mechanical means to the Royal Navy. The plans were accepted and he was placed in charge of installing the machines at Portsmouth Dockyard. His son, Isambard Kingdom Brunel, was born in Portsmouth in 1806. He studied architecture in France and then joined his father's engineering business during the early stages of construction of the Thames Tunnel. He went on to become the country's leading engineer through his work on bridges, the Great Western Railway and the steamships Great Western, Great Britain *and* Great Eastern.

THE VICTORIAN DOCKYARD

The Victorian era brought enormous expansion and change to the dockyard, taking in the huge expanse of land to the north east (much of it reclaimed from mudflats) to create Nos 2 and 3 Basins and the surrounding dry docks and workshops. Sail was giving way to steam and wood to iron, requiring extensive new facilities, technologies and crafts. In 1845 there were still 276 sailing warships in the Navy, including eighty-seven ships-of-the-line, augmented by thirty-seven steam warships (none of which were ships-of-the-line). However, by 1860, sixty-four of the ninety ships-of-the-line were steam-assisted, and steam predominated in the fleet of 323 frigates, sloops and smaller vessels. In this era over half of the fleet was in 'ordinary', i.e. in reserve, including most of the sailing ships. Unlike previous developments to the Dockyard, which had been prompted by wars, it was now technology that was driving change. Also, the Navy was growing in size to police the world-wide territories of the British Empire, and the naval ambitions of France remained a factor.

In 1848, Queen Victoria opened the new Steam Basin (now No.2 Basin) to the north of the old dockyard area. Excavation of the non-tidal basin had employed 1,200 convicts from hulks moored in the harbour, as well as 1,050 wage labourers, and the work took five years to complete. At the same time, two new dry docks (Nos 7 and 8) and a large Steam Factory were built, and were soon complemented by the Iron Foundry, Steam Smithery, and a further dry dock (No.10). One of the cranes built to serve the Steam Basin was the first steam-powered crane in the Dockyard, whilst the two others were still manually operated. Two months before the Steam Basin opened the last sailing ship to be built at Portsmouth was launched. She was the *Leander,* a 50-gun Fourth Rate.

The Steam Factory, built along the west side of the Steam Basin, was a huge engineering workshop containing a wide range of machining and fabrication operations. Completed in 1849, it transformed the Dockyard's capabilities, harnessing the tools of the Industrial Revolution. Its appearance is impressive, the design being an architectural riposte to the storehouses being built by the French Navy at Cherbourg. Over 600ft long, with two storeys, it is built of red brick offset by Portland stone cornices and pedimented bays.

A 1904 view of the entrance to the dockyard Camber, showing Kings Stairs. (Portsmouth City Libraries)

The Iron Foundry facing No.8 Dock was built in a similar style, whilst a new Smithery was erected behind the Steam Factory, using a more economical metal frame clad with corrugated iron sheeting.

Although most of the new facilities were built around the Steam Basin in the 1840s, the elegant new Boat Storehouse, now No.6 Boathouse, was constructed in the older part of the dockyard. Beneath its traditional buff-coloured brick exterior is a frame of iron columns and girders. It can be seen on the right behind the Boat Pond on the road between the Main Gate and the *Victory*. Boats could be hauled from the Pond on rails through the three large arched doors on the front of the building.

The commissioning of HMS *Warrior* in 1860 meant that even these new facilities were inadequate for the new generation of large ironclad battleships. A new, longer, drydock (No.11) was excavated alongside the Steam Basin and completed in 1863 but this was only a stopgap before much larger provision could be made. In 1867 the construction of a tidal basin leading to two large locks, which gave entry to three new interlinked non-tidal basins and three dry docks, was approved. The Great Extension, as it was called, increased the total size of the yard from 116 to 300 acres. About 95 acres of the new land was subject to tidal conditions, necessitating the building of a dam 4,100ft long and the pumping dry of the enclosed area. The extension project employed some 1,500 workers and 800 convicts, the latter being housed in a specially-built prison just outside the dockyard wall. Clay dredged from the excavations was utilised in the large brickworks which at one point made 20 million bricks a year. The other excavated material was transported to an exposed mudbank nearby, becoming Whale Island, home to the Navy's gunnery school (HMS *Excellent)*. The dockyard extension was officially opened in 1876 on the same day that the appropriately named battleship *Inflexible* was launched at No.5 Slip. She had 24in

The Tidal Basin in 1910, with the Steam Factory in the background. (Portsmouth City Museums)

The launch of the battleship *Dreadnought* on No.5 Slip. She was built in a record twelve months as a prestige exercise intended to impress the German Navy. Large amounts of overtime were paid to the dockyard workers, who worked a 69 hour week instead of their usual 48 hours. From the laying of the keel plates to the launch on 10 February 1906 took just eighteen weeks. Fitting out and the official steam trials took a further eight months. (Portsmouth City Libraries)

Visit of the King and Queen of Portugal, South Railway Jetty, 1904. (Portsmouth City Libraries)

armour, the thickest ever mounted on a ship. Two additional larger dry docks (Nos 14 and 15) were not completed until 1896 and were big enough to take the late Victorian classes of battleship.

In the 1860s Portsmouth was still building wooden-hulled ships. It was not until 1871, eleven years after the *Warrior* was launched, that the yard launched its first large iron-hulled warship – HMS *Devastation,* and like *Warrior* she was a milestone in capital ship development. She was the first capital ship to dispense with sails altogether and had twelve-inch guns mounted in turrets on the top of the hull, rather than the broadside arrangement of guns mounted internally on carriages which the *Warrior* still had.

Battleship evolution took another leap forward with the completion at Portsmouth in 1906 of HMS *Dreadnought,* the first to be powered by steam turbines. This initiated the great arms race between Britain and Germany and rendered the earlier Edwardian and late Victorian battleships obsolete. Larger, faster and more heavily armed, the Dreadnoughts were once again pushing the dockyard's capacity to its limits. Larger dry-docking facilities were needed, so two new locks (C and D) were built. This also allowed easier access for large ships to No.3 Basin (which had been created through the combining of the three newest basins in the Great Extension). As the fleet of Dreadnoughts was growing rapidly the newest dry docks, Nos 14 and 15, were lengthened. Portsmouth's pre-eminence as a dockyard was unquestionable. The first of each new class of Dreadnoughts was built there – *Dreadnought* herself being followed by *Bellerophon* (1907), *St Vincent* (1908), *Neptune* (1909), *Orion* (1910), *King George V* (1911), *Iron Duke* (1912), *Queen Elizabeth* (1913) and *Royal Sovereign* (1915). In July 1914, just before the outbreak of the First World War, there

The Floating Dock being brought into Portsmouth Harbour, 1912. At the time it was the world's largest floating dock and could easily accommodate the largest Dreadnoughts of the era. A jetty was built in the Dockyard at the eastern end of Fountain Lake with a railway so that repair materials could be brought alongside. With this addition the Dockyard could dock five Dreadnoughts at any one time. The floating dock was finally towed away in 1939 to Malta for further service. Other floating docks followed at Portsmouth and a number were built in the Dockyard. (Portsmouth City Libraries)

was a Review of the Fleet at Spithead where the newly completed *Iron Duke* joined fifty-four other battleships and four battlecruisers, plus a host of cruisers, destroyers, submarines, torpedo boats, in a forbidding spectacle of sea power that eclipsed all previous Fleet Reviews at Spithead. When the ships dispersed the First Fleet sailed north to its wartime anchorage at Scapa Flow.

TWO WORLD WARS — AND AFTER

The Dockyard was at its busiest ever in the two World Wars. The mobilisation of the Reserve Fleet, shipbuilding, conversion of merchant ships for warfare, and the repair and maintenance of the vastly expanded fleet provided work for 23,000 employees in the First World War and 25,000 in the Second. Between 1914 and 1918 the yard refitted 1,200 vessels including forty battleships, twenty-five cruisers, 400 destroyers, 150 torpedo boats and twenty submarines. At this time it also built its first submarines. There was one unsuccessful Zeppelin attack on the Dockyard, which emerged unscathed.

In the Second World War the yard was not so lucky, suffering extensive damage under heavy bombing. Capital ships were moved away from Portsmouth, but even so 2,548 vessels were repaired or refitted there. Shipbuilding continued with the construction of the cruiser *Sirius* and the submarines *Tireless* and *Token*. In 1944 Portsmouth became the leading base for assembly and preparations for the D-Day landings in Normandy. The operations were controlled from HMS *Dryad*, the Navigation School at Southwick, by General Eisenhower, the Supreme Allied Commander. Stokes Bay, Lee-on-Solent, Hardway and Gosport town provided major points for embarkation of the troops into their landing craft.

After the war there was inevitable contraction of the dockyard, but the routine refitting work was augmented in the 1950s and 1960s by major modernisation and conversion work on war built ships such as the aircraft carriers *Victorious* and *Triumph*, the cruiser *Blake*, the destroyers *Agincourt* and *Matapan*, and A and T class submarines. However, it was later decided that in most cases it was more economical to build new ships than carry out expensive mid-life modernisations. For fifteen years between 1953 and 1968 there was also a busy programme of shipbuilding at the Dockyard, with the construction of the frigates *Leopard*, *Rhyl*, *Nubian*, *Sirius* and *Andromeda*. By 1978 the workforce had reduced to 8,325 and in the 1981 Defence Review a rundown of Portsmouth Dockyard was announced by the Conservative Government, together with the closure of Chatham and Gibraltar Dockyards.

A view across Locks C and D towards Whale Island, taken in 1914. (Portsmouth City Libraries)

The Dido-class cruiser *Sirius* was completed at Portsmouth in 1942 and had a distinguished war career, obtaining battle honours for the Arctic, Malta Convoys, Mediterranean, North Africa, Sicily, Salerno, the Aegean, Normandy and South of France. After the war she served in the Home Fleet until being placed in reserve at Portsmouth in 1949. She was broken up in 1956. (Dave Page Collection)

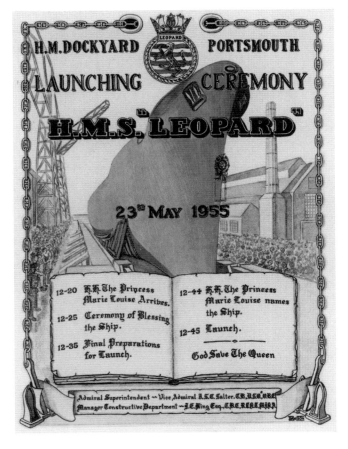

Above: The submarine *Tireless*, completed at Portsmouth in 1945. She is shown here in her original appearance, before modernization in 1950. Her final service was at Gosport in the First Submarine Squadron. She was broken up in 1968. (Dave Page Collection)

Left: Launch of the frigate *Leopard* in 1955. She was the first post-war ship to be built at the yard.

HMS *Leopard* seen leaving Portsmouth in July 1968. (Author)

The Portsmouth-built Leander class frigate *Sirius* seen entering Portsmouth Harbour in August 1968. (Author)

The Leander class frigate *Andromeda* fitting out in No.2 Basin at Portsmouth in August 1968. She was the last warship to be built by the Royal Dockyard, and was later in action in the Falklands War. (Author)

The cruiser *Blake* seen in August 1968 in dockyard hands for her conversion to carry helicopters. (Author)

Harbour view with King George V class battleship at the South Railway Jetty, *c.* 1950.

On Friday 2 April 1982, every member of the dockyard staff at Portsmouth received a letter informing them of the future redundancies. On the same day, came news of the Argentinian invasion of the Falkland Islands. This gave the dockyard a temporary reprieve as the urgent work of preparing ships for the Falklands Task Force was immediately started. The assault ship *Intrepid* had been paid off and was being de-stored for possible sale, whilst the aircraft carrier *Hermes* was undergoing a dockyard-assisted maintenance period, and *Invincible* was having operational defects put right whilst her crew were on Easter leave. That weekend, aircraft were flown aboard *Hermes* and *Invincible* as they were stored, loaded with armaments and fuelled, and the essential maintenance tasks were completed. On Monday 5 April, just three days after the decision to send a Task Force, they sailed from the port for the South Atlantic. Other ships prepared at Portsmouth for the Falklands included the assault ship *Fearless* (as well as *Intrepid*), the destroyer *Bristol*, the frigate *Diomede*, the survey ships *Hydra* and *Hecla* – which were converted into hospital ships, the patrol ships *Leeds Castle* and *Dumbarton Castle*, and a number of Royal Fleet Auxiliaries, one of which, the *Stromness*, had been paid off for disposal. Work was brought forward to prepare other ships for further Falklands operations, including the carrier *Illustrious*, and the destroyers *Fife, Newcastle, Liverpool, Southampton* and *Birmingham*. Eighteen merchant ships that were taken up by the Navy for support roles were also prepared for their new duties at the dockyard. After the conflict, damage repairs were undertaken on the destroyers *Glamorgan, Antrim* and *Glasgow*, and the submarine *Onyx*.

With the end of the Falklands emergency the run down of the yard began. In 1984 the Royal Dockyard was renamed the Naval Base, and the Fleet Maintenance and Repair Organisation took over a reduced volume of ship refitting and repair, with a workforce of just 1,400.

PORTSMOUTH NAVAL BASE

Portsmouth Naval Base is one of three Royal Navy bases – the others being Devonport and Clyde (principally Faslane). It is the home to over half of the surface fleet, including the three aircraft carriers, all of the Type 42 destroyers, half of the Type 23 frigates, two mine countermeasure squadrons, the Fishery Protection Squadron, and a number of patrol vessels. The two new large aircraft carriers and the Type 45 *Daring* class destroyers will also be based at Portsmouth, replacing the *Invincible* class and the Type 42s. To accommodate the new carriers a massive upgrade of the base is planned. This will include dredging a deeper channel on both sides of the harbour mouth, and providing a deep water mooring for the carriers off Stokes Bay. The South Railway Jetty and Fountain Lake Jetty will be rebuilt, access to No.3 Basin will be improved, and the base's facilities will be upgraded. These developments appear to assure the future of the base which is still the city's largest direct and indirect employer.

Within the base is the Royal Naval Supply Depot which holds and distributes eighty per cent of the non-explosive stores used by the surface fleet. There is no longer a Royal Dockyard: the modern parts of the yard that are still used for warship repair and refitting are now operated by Fleet Support Ltd (FSL), a private sector Joint Venture between BAE Systems and the VT Group. The company's work has been expanded to include the refitting of commercial ships such as cross-Channel and Isle of Wight ferries, British Antarctic Survey ships, and the modernization of redundant Royal Navy ships which have been sold to other navies. FSL's work is centred around No.3 Basin with the associated dry docks (Nos 11-15) and locks. After a gap of thirty-five years shipbuilding has returned to the dockyard. The VT Group (formerly Vosper Thornycroft) has relocated its shipbuilding activity from Woolston (near Southampton) to the base and is involved in the construction of modules for the *Daring* class destroyers.

The Type 23 frigate HMS *Richmond* receiving attention in No.12 Dock, August 1998. (Author)

The patrol ship *Guernsey* at the south Railway Jetty, abreast of the Railway Shelter (1893) constructed for Queen Victoria. (Author)

MARY ROSE

On 19 July 1545, a French invasion fleet was engaged by a fleet of English ships including the flagship *Henry Grace a Dieu* at Spithead. At the newly-built Southsea Castle, King Henry VIII watched in horror as the leading English ship, the *Mary Rose* – reputedly his favourite ship – sank before his eyes. She was to lie on the seabed for over 400 years before her remains were raised in 1982.

The *Mary Rose* was built between 1510-1511 in the first dry dock at Portsmouth. She was named after Henry's favourite sister, Mary, and his family emblem, the Tudor rose. A successful ship, she was designed to fight at close range, by closing with the enemy before firing her guns and then coming alongside to allow the soldiers she was carrying to board and capture the enemy ship using hand-to-hand fighting. Her heaviest guns, mounted low in the stern, were mainly used to bombard shore positions. She fought in battles against the French at Brest and Cherbourg during the First French War between 1512 and 1514, and against the Scots at Newcastle in 1513. In the Second French War (1522-1525) she was in action again, but her nemesis was in the next war with France, which started in 1543. The French had built up a huge armada of 235 vessels in Le Havre and in 1545 that fleet sailed for England hoping to capture the Isle of Wight to use as a base to invade the mainland. The King was aboard the flagship *Henry Grace a Dieu* when the first French ships were sighted rounding Bembridge Point, but was taken ashore to Southsea. The French were met by eighty English ships which had gathered at Portsmouth, with another sixty on their way from the west country. Very light winds made engagement between the two fleets difficult. Lord de Lisle, in the English flagship, ordered his forward ships to try and lure the enemy under the powerful guns of Southsea Castle. The *Mary Rose*, which had excellent sailing qualities, was soon ahead of the others. It was reported that she fired a starboard broadside and then tacked to enable her port broadside to be fired. Unfortunately, the gun port lids on the port side were not closed and water rushed in as the ship heeled to port following a sudden gust of wind. It seems that her crew contained too many senior mariners, including ships' masters, who would not take orders from one

A bronze culverin retrieved from the *Mary Rose* site, on display in the Mary Rose Museum. The original gun has acquired a new elm carriage. (Author)

another and this contributed to the error. The ship sank with the reported loss of over 500 lives, there being only twenty-five sailors and a few personal servants who survived. Unable to properly engage the English, the French turned away and later made landings on the Isle of Wight at Sandown, Shanklin, Bonchurch and Nettlestone, but withdrew in the face of the English forces on the island.

Following her sinking, unsuccessful attempts were made by expert Venetian salvors to raise the *Mary Rose*, but some of the guns, and the masts and rigging, were recovered by them. In 1836 the wreck was located by divers and a bronze cannon was salved.

Facts and Figures

As built, the *Mary Rose* was listed as 500 tons. She underwent two refits and it is believed that in the second (around 1536) she was rebuilt and uprated to 700 tons. Her hull was strengthened by the addition of diagonal braces between the orlop (lowest) deck and the hold. She was given a powerful broadside battery of heavy cannon which was capable of inflicting serious damage on other ships at a distance. She was equipped to fire her ahead weapons (which were actually mounted on the aftercastle and fired off-centre) before turning to fire first a broadside, then to fire astern, and finally to fire the other broadside. She then made off to reload and other ships took her place. This new emphasis on artillery meant that she was a prototype for the large galleons of the late sixteenth century which defeated the Spanish Armada. Her rebuild helps explain why the only contemporary painting of the *Mary Rose* shows differences from the hull that was lifted at Spithead.

Mary Rose had a keel length of 32m, a waterline length of about 38.5m and an overall length of about 45m including the bowsprit. Her beam was 11.66m and her draught about 4.6m. The height of the aftercastle, seen on the preserved section, was 14m. She had four masts – the fore and main being square rigged, whilst the mizzen and bonaventure were lateen rigged (triangular fore and aft sails which helped the ship sail to windward).

At the time of her loss her armament consisted of: fifteen heavy, cast bronze, muzzle loading guns; twenty-four heavy, wrought iron, breech loading guns; and thirty wrought iron, breech loading swivel guns.

In addition to the cannon her crew carried fifty handguns, 250 longbows, 300 pole arms, 480 darts to throw from the fighting tops and a large number of arrows.

Her crew was listed in 1545 as 200 mariners, 185 soldiers and thirty gunners, although one account says there were over 700 men on board when she sank.

King Henry VIII

With the news that a French invasion fleet was in the Channel, Henry came to Portsmouth on 15 July 1545 to prepare for the French attack and possible landing. Aged fifty-four, he was now an enormous man as a result of his excessive eating and drinking. He had to be hoisted on to his horse, and when indoors was carried about in a chair and hauled upstairs by machinery. As he rode towards Southsea Castle on 19 July he was dressed

The only surviving contemporary illustration of the *Mary Rose* appeared in the Anthony Roll, a list of the King's ships published in 1546, a year after the loss of the ship. Her name was spelled *Mary Roase*. (Master and Fellows of Magdelene College, Cambridge)

Another view of the hull showing the weather deck, upper deck, castle deck, sterncastle and main deck (all labelled) and, below the main deck, the orlop deck. (The Mary Rose Trust)

not in wide-girthed armour but in his full Renaissance finery. On that day there was little wind, so the English ships emerging from Portsmouth Harbour were moving slowly. The fleet was led by the Henry Grace a Dieu (or the Great Harry as she was known), but Henry would also have recognised the Mary Rose, her pennons rustling in the light air, her guns protruding their ports in readiness for battle. Seeing her forge ahead of the fleet he must have been greatly shocked to witness the catastrophe of her sinking. The King was already ageing, unwell, worn down by endless foreign wars, and close to bankruptcy himself. The loss of his favourite ship must have come as another blow, perhaps hastening his decline. He was nearing the end of his reign and died eighteen months later.

Restoration of the Mary Rose

In the 1960s attempts were made to locate the wreck, and in 1967, using sonar, a discontinuity was found in the silt that was to prove to be the remains of the *Mary Rose* hull. In 1979 the Mary Rose Trust was formed to raise the wreck and over the next three years many timbers and artefacts were recovered by divers whilst the site was excavated and the starboard side of the hull was prepared for lifting. This was the side that had lain in the silt of the seabed, the port side having been destroyed through exposure to currents and marine organisms. Steel cables were attached to the 280-ton hull structure, which was then lifted onto a specially shaped cradle. The cradle was lifted above the surface on 11 October 1982 and placed on the deck of a barge ready to be towed into Portsmouth Harbour.

The hull section can now be seen in the historic No.3 dry dock (built in 1799) which has been covered with an insulated roof. The hull still sits in the cradle used in the lifting

Part of the Cowdray Engraving showing the sinking of the *Mary Rose*. Her topmasts can be seen above Southsea Castle where King Henry VIII can be seen on horseback. On the left is part of the French fleet whilst on the right the English fleet is seen with the *Henry Grace a Dieu* in the van.

operation, and is undergoing restoration. Many timbers salvaged from the wreck site have been returned to their original positions, and the process of conserving the hull continues. Initially the hull was continuously sprayed with chilled fresh water, to control marine organism growth and maintain humidity. After twelve years polyethylene glycol (PEG) was introduced into the spray system. This wax solution penetrated the timber cells over seven years, replacing the water throughout the timber thickness. Then, in 2003, a different grade of PEG was introduced, to penetrate only the outer walls of the timber. This will eventually be allowed to dry and solidify, providing mechanical support to the fragile cell walls of the timber. Once this process is complete the hull will be able to be displayed in an open museum environment. This could be in around 2015. The experience of restoring the *Vasa*, a Swedish full-rigged warship which sank on her maiden voyage in 1628 has informed the process on *Mary Rose*. The *Vasa* was raised in 1961 and is now on open display in Stockholm.

Divers at the *Mary Rose* site brought 19,000 objects to the surface, of which 11,000 have been conserved or restored. Mostly undisturbed for four centuries, they have given an unparalleled insight into Tudor life as it was on the day that the ship sank – revealing a whole Tudor world, in a way that excavation of land sites cannot equal. A total of 172 yew longbows were found as well as 2,300 arrows, mostly made from poplar with an iron head, and twenty-five cannon. The remains of 179 men were found – they were mostly aged in their twenties and had healthy teeth and bones. Symbolically, one unknown mariner was laid to rest in a grave inside Portsmouth Cathedral.

In the Mary Rose Museum in the Historic Dockyard many of the artefacts recovered from the site can be seen. These include tableware, cutlery, candleholders, cooking pots, musical instruments, a backgammon set, book covers, quill pens and inkpots together with items of clothing and shoes. As well as cannons and shot, there are swords, arrows and longbows, navigation instruments and many other items of equipment and tooling. A fighting top (possibly intended to be the highest of those on the main mast) was found and has been restored – this and some other items of rigging were in storage below deck and escaped salvage by the Venetian divers. A replica section of the main and upper deck has been constructed in the museum and is fitted with original bronze and iron guns which were found protruding through the open gun ports when the ship was excavated. Only one contemporary painting of the *Mary Rose* exists, in the Anthony Roll, a list of King Henry VIII's ships that was completed in 1546. This illustration differs in some respects from the excavated hull. Another illustration, the Cowdray Engraving, shows the scene at Southsea and Spithead as the *Mary Rose* sank. It is an eighteenth century engraving based on a Tudor wall painting, now lost, that once belonged to Cowdray House in Sussex.

HMS VICTORY

HMS *Victory* is a remarkable emblem of the Royal Navy's success in the age of fighting sailing ships. The oldest commissioned warship in the world, she is the only surviving three-decked ship of the line and has been restored to magnificent condition. No first time visitor to Portsmouth should omit a tour around her. Open every day, except for Christmas Day, over 350,000 people a year visit her. In the summer months a group of about twenty-five visitors starts a guided tour every five minutes.

That she has survived to this day is probably attributable to three things. Firstly, her massive oak construction: she was laid down in a dry dock at Chatham Dockyard on 23 July 1759, but not floated-out (launched) until 7 May 1765. Her timbers were thus fully seasoned by the time she entered the water. Secondly, she had a long operational career. *Victory* represented the zenith of ship-of-the-line design, and although forty years old when she fought at Trafalgar she was still a powerful and competitive force. When she retired from active service she was nearly fifty years old. Even so, her design was used as the basis of two new Second Rates – the *London* of 1810 and the *Princess Charlotte* of 1825. Thirdly, having been Nelson's flagship at Trafalgar, probably the Navy's most proud victory, she was retained in commission in harbour roles at Portsmouth long after her contemporaries were scrapped. *Victory* is now the flagship of the Second Sea Lord and Commander-in-Chief Naval Home Command and can be seen flying the White Ensign in No.2 dry dock where she has lain since 1922. Her crew still consists of Officers and Ratings of the Royal Navy and she has been commanded by about eighty different admirals in her life. As exhibited she has been restored to her Trafalgar appearance. The black and yellow hull colours of 1800 were adapted by Nelson who ordered the gunport lids to be painted black producing the distinctive chequer pattern which became standard in the Royal Navy thereafter.

HMS *Victory* with the submarine B1 alongside.

HMS *Victory*, a broadside view. (Author)

HMS VICTORY —
FACTS AND FIGURES

Length: 69.0m/226ft 6in overall (including bowsprit), 56.6m/186ft on lower gun deck.
Beam: 15.7m/51ft 10in. Displacement: 3,556 tonnes/3,500 tons

Hull thickness at waterline: approx. 0.6m/2ft. Hull constructed from approximately 6,000 trees, 90% of which was oak, also elm (keel) and fir, pine and spruce (masts and yards). This equates to 100 acres (40 hectares) of woodland.

Masts (with exception of bowsprit, heights are taken from waterline):
Bowsprit: 33.5m/110ft. Foremast: 55.4m/182ft. Main mast: 62.4m/205ft
Mizzen mast: 46.3m/152ft. Main yard: 31.0m/102ft

Sails: 37 sails with total area 5,468 square metres/6,510 square yards.
Rigging: A total of 42 km/26 miles of cordage was used to rig the ship. 768 elm or ash blocks were used in the rigging. (A further 628 were used for the gun carriages).
Speed: Maximum approx. 10 knots. Normal fair weather 8 knots.

Crew: 821 including Vice-Admiral Lord Nelson, at the Battle of Trafalgar. This included 146 marines. There were ten ship's officers including Captain Hardy, and a captain and three lieutenants of the marines. The crew was comprised of twenty-two different nationalities including four French! The oldest was Walter Burke aged 67, the youngest was Thomas Twitchet aged 12.

The decorated stern galleries of the *Victory*. (Author)

VICTORY'S GUNS

Victory was a First Rate, the largest of only four such ships in the fleet at the time of her completion. First Rates had 100 guns or more, and were usually employed as senior flagships. Third Rates – the most numerous ships-of-the-line – had between 64 and 80 guns. *Victory* was completed with 100 guns, of four different types, the heaviest being 42-pounders (referring to weight of the iron roundshot). These were all muzzle loading guns and were arranged over three decks, with the heaviest on the lower deck and the lightest on the upper deck to help preserve a low centre of gravity. By the time of Trafalgar, the number of guns was 104, but the original 42-pounders had been replaced by 32-pounders before the ship commissioned in 1778 because they were cumbersome (requiring a larger crew) and had a slow firing rate. Although twelve Napoleonic-era iron guns remain on the ship today they are unlikely to be those used at Trafalgar because the originals were removed in 1806 and the existing ones were fitted in 1808.

Each 32-pounder required a crew of thirteen and the emphasis was on rapid firing rather than accuracy. It had a maximum range of 2,366m (2,600yds) though in action ships often engaged at close quarters. A well-trained crew might fire their gun every two minutes. Broadsides would be directed at either the rigging (favoured by the French, to disable the ship), or hull (favoured by the British who wished to overcome the ship at short range prior to boarding and taking the enemy ship as a prize). At close range the powder charge would be reduced to prevent the ball passing right through the hull of the enemy vessel. Bar shot and chain shot was also used to cut through rigging and spars. At Trafalgar, two heavier guns, 68-pounder carronades, were carried on the forecastle. These were low velocity close-range weapons. The first shot fired by the *Victory* at Trafalgar was from the port side carronade, hitting the stern of the French flagship *Bucentaure*.

A 32-pounder gun, and mess area, on the lower deck of *Victory*. The planking on this deck is original. (Author)

24-pounders, middle gun deck HMS *Victory*. (Author)

Armament at Trafalgar

Lower gun deck: 30 x 32-pounder
Middle gun deck: 28 x 24-pounder
Upper gun deck: 30 x 12-pounder (long)
Quarterdeck: 12 x 12-pounder (short)
Forecastle: 2 x 12-pounder (medium), 2 x 68-pounder carronade.

VICTORY'S SERVICE CAREER

Following her completion in 1765 *Victory* undertook sea trials but was then placed in 'Ordinary' (reserve) as Britain was at peace with France following the end of the Seven Years War in 1763. In 1778, after France had joined the American War of Independence, she was commissioned into the Channel Fleet as the flagship of Admiral Keppel and thereafter was nearly always an admiral's flagship. In 1780 her hull was sheathed in copper sheeting below the waterline to combat the teredo worm which bored into wooden ships' hulls. In 1781, as Admiral Kempenfelt's flagship, she led a squadron which intercepted a French fleet off Ushant, in the Bay of Biscay. Fourteen French ships of the line were escorting a large convoy of military transports bound for the West Indies. Kempenfelt caught the convoy to windward of its escorts and was able to capture fifteen transports whilst the remainder of the fleet scattered. In April 1782, under the flag of Lord Howe, *Victory* took part in action off Cape Spartel and the Relief of Gibraltar, when Howe successfully evaded the Franco-Spanish fleet and delivered into Gibraltar the thirty merchantmen he was escorting. In November 1782 she paid off for a refit at Portsmouth before entering Ordinary again. In 1787 she was made ready for service, due to a brief crisis with the Netherlands, but returned to reserve. In 1790 she was commissioned as Lord Hood's flagship in the Channel Fleet.

After a refit in 1792 *Victory* again became the flagship of Lord Hood in 1793 at the start of the French Revolutionary War. Hood, who was now in command of the Mediterranean Fleet, captured Toulon briefly and destroyed nine French ships of the line. The fleet then captured, but was unable to hold, the island of Corsica. Horatio Nelson, then a young captain commanding the *Agamemnon*, lost the sight of his right eye in this action. In December 1794 *Victory* returned to Portsmouth and entered the dockyard for repairs and updating. In July 1795 she returned to the Mediterranean as the flagship of Rear Admiral Sir John Man, and was in action with the French off Hyeres. In December Admiral Sir John Jervis transferred his flag to her and in 1796 she was part of a blockade of Toulon.

Above: The quarterdeck on HMS *Victory*. (Author)

Right: A view of the after gun decks with a boat lowered. (Author)

Victory in dry dock, flying the Trafalgar signal.

In 1797, still under Jervis, *Victory* and fourteen other ships-of-the-line engaged a Spanish fleet of twenty-seven ships of the line off Cape St Vincent. Jervis secured a notable victory, in which Nelson, commanding the *Captain*, played an audacious part – capturing two Spanish ships and earning himself a knighthood and promotion to Rear-Admiral. *Victory* came home to pay off at Chatham and became a hospital ship for prisoners-of-war on the Medway. This could have spelt the end of her active service. However, there was a shortage of First Rates and in 1800 she entered a major refit, and was recommissioned in 1803 for further service in the Mediterranean. War was declared with France that year on 18 May and *Victory* sailed from Portsmouth on 20 May with Lord Nelson aboard, flying his flag as the newly-appointed Commander-in-Chief of the Mediterranean Fleet. Nelson blockaded Toulon, from which the French Fleet eventually escaped in May 1805 whilst Nelson's main fleet was at Sardinia. Chased by Nelson to the West Indies and back, the French were then bottled up in Cadiz. Nelson briefly returned to Portsmouth in *Victory* in August 1805. He sailed from there for the last time on 15 September, for Cadiz, from where he pursued the French and Spanish to the engagement off Cape Trafalgar.

THE BATTLE OF TRAFALGAR

Admiral Villeneuve, commanding the combined Franco-Spanish fleet in Cadiz, was criticised by Napoleon for failing to decisively engage the British, and a replacement admiral was despatched to take over his command. Villeneuve acted, sailing from Cadiz on 19 October 1805 with thirty-three ships. Early on the next morning he was sighted by Nelson's frigates and pursued by the British fleet as they made for the Straits of Gibraltar. At 6.10 on the morning of 21 October Nelson signalled from the *Victory* to his fleet to form the Order of Sailing in Two Columns. One column of twelve ships was led by the *Victory*, whilst to leeward another column, of fifteen ships, was led by Admiral Collingwood in *Royal Sovereign*. Nelson planned that his two columns would allow him to cut the enemy line at two points. At 6.22 he signalled 'Prepare for Battle'. Villeneuve wore his ships round so that they headed roughly NNW and the British steered towards the North East to cut off access to Cadiz. Ahead and to leeward of them lay the French and Spanish ships, arranged in two lines which converged to present a crescent like formation.

In light winds, the first engagement was between the *Fourgueux* and the *Royal Sovereign*, at about 11.30. At 11.48 Nelson made his famous signal 'England Expects That Every Man Will Do His Duty'. Within minutes *Victory* was under fire from all quarters, suffering heavy losses. Whilst *Royal Sovereign* fought the Spanish flagship *Santa Ana, Victory* steered towards the giant *Santissima Trinidad,* but then identified the *Bucentaure* as Villeneuve's flagship and fired her first shots at point blank range. The French ship was effectively disabled, and *Victory* then broke through the enemy line, moving alongside the *Redoutable* which had been close to the *Bucentaure.* The upper decks of the two ships became a maelstrom of shot and carnage. Nelson, in full uniform on the quarterdeck of the *Victory*, was targeted at 1.15 p.m. by a musketeer in the mizzentop of *Redoutable,* 15 metres above him. A musket ball entered his left breast and he fell, mortally wounded. *Temeraire* came to *Victory's* assistance and *Redoutable* was forced to strike her colours, with over 300 dead.

The battle continued until about 4.30 p.m. Nelson's strategy of splitting the enemy into three parts had succeeded: Villeneuve had surrendered, seventeen enemy ships were

A deck view on *Victory*, also showing the fighting tops. (Author)

captured as prizes and one sank. Four of the surviving ships were taken two days later, whilst the remainder retreated to Cadiz. The *Santa Ana* was recovered by the Spaniards from her small prize crew, and other prizes foundered or were wrecked in the gales which followed the battle. As a result only four prizes were brought home by the British. All of the British ships survived, though many were dismasted or heavily damaged. Nelson died a hero's death, breathing his last at 4.30 p.m. He was one of fifty-seven to die on the *Victory*, more than on any other British ship. In all 449 men died in the British fleet, but losses on the Franco-Spanish fleet were much higher – it is estimated that about 4,400 perished and thousands were taken prisoner. The captured Villeneuve was repatriated the following year, but committed suicide – 'a gallant man but without talent' remarked Napoleon. Britain's naval supremacy was once again assured, and the threat of invasion by the French was averted. Trafalgar was one of the most decisive and famous of all naval battles.

The order in which the British Squadron attacked the Combined Fleets

VAN: *Victory, Temeraire, Neptune, Conqueror, Leviathan, Ajax, Orion, Agamemnon, Minotaur, Spartiate, Britannia,* and *Africa,* plus the frigates *Euryalus, Sirius, Phoebe,* and *Naiad,* and the schooner *Pickle.*

REAR: *Royal Sovereign, Mars, Belleisle, Tonnant, Bellerophon, Colossus, Achille, Polyphemus, Revenge, Swiftsure, Defence, Thunderer, Defiance, Prince* and *Dreadnought.*

HMS VICTORY AFTER TRAFALGAR

Victory arrived home at Portsmouth on 4 December 1805 under jury rig, with Nelson's body. After urgent repairs she sailed to the Thames, arriving at Sheerness on 22 December. There the body was transferred to a yacht for passage to Greenwich. *Victory* paid off at Chatham the following month for a major refit and repairs and then entered reserve on the Medway. She was recommissioned in 1808 and her last seagoing service was in the Baltic, as flagship of Rear Admiral de Saumarez, and off the coasts of Spain. She was involved in a number of skirmishes with the Danes in the Baltic and transported troops to and from the Iberian Peninsula in support of Wellington.

She paid off into reserve at Portsmouth in 1812, and from 1813 to 1816 underwent major repairs and reconstruction. After further spell in Ordinary she became flagship at Portsmouth of successively the Port Admiral in 1825, the Admiral Superintendent of the Dockyard in 1837, and the Commander-in-Chief, Home Fleet, in 1847. In 1869 she paid off and was used for accommodation and storage as a tender to the new flagship, the *Duke of Wellington*. In 1887 her lower masts, which had rotted, were replaced by lighter hollow iron masts removed from the armoured frigate *Shah*, and thus date from that ship's construction in 1870. In 1899 the custom of flying Nelson's 'England Expects' signal from her masts on Trafalgar Day (21 October) was started. In 1903 the battleship *Neptune*, which was leaving harbour under tow bound for the shipbreakers, broke loose from her tugs and collided with the *Victory*. She so badly damaged her that she began to sink and had to be dry-docked for repairs. Together with the general deterioration over time to the fabric of the ship, this incident raised questions about her future but nothing was resolved before World War One and *Victory* remained afloat in Portsmouth Harbour. In 1921 a report on the ship's condition was prepared by the Society for Nautical Research and passed to the Admiralty. It indicated that unless something was done the days of the ship were numbered. The Admiralty agreed to make a permanent dry dock available and the Society launched a public appeal to fund the ship's restoration. In December 1921 *Victory* was moved into No.1 Basin to prepare her for docking, and the following month was moved to her present

Photographed on the centennial anniversary of Trafalgar, 21 October 1905, HMS *Victory* was still afloat in Portsmouth Harbour and is flying Nelson's famous signal 'England expects that every man will do his duty.' Alongside her is the submarine *D1*. (Portsmouth City Libraries)

dry dock to commence restoration. A steel cradle was fabricated to support her hull. On 8 April 1925 she was refloated for the last time to adjust the cradle so that her waterline was level with the top of the dock, allowing her lines to be seen to the best advantage.

On 17 July 1928, King George V visited Portsmouth to open the ship to the public. During the Second World War she was closed to visitors and stripped of her upper masts and rigging. She was used for a time as an accommodation ship for junior ranks from the Royal Naval Barracks, and for gunners of the Portsmouth anti-aircraft defences. In 1941 she narrowly escaped destruction in a night-time raid when a 500lb high explosive bomb fell into the dry dock and burst under her port bow, blowing a hole 8ft x 15ft in the ship's side. Since the war continuous restoration and maintenance has been necessary. The Death Watch beetle, a notorious pest of structural oak woodwork, had been discovered in 1932 and between 1954 and 1956 a programme of fumigation was carried out but the problem re-emerged in the 1970s so an annual treatment using insecticide emulsion and smoke was introduced. On enclosed timbers the replacement of decayed oak by teak and iroko has also helped reduce the beetle problem. Many of the remaining wooden spars, which were difficult to repair, were replaced with mild steel in the seventies though Douglas fir continues to be used for some.

In 2004 the hold and the grand magazine were opened to the public for the first time. The hold is a large area below the orlop deck (the deck on which Nelson died) that held shingle ballast and ship's stores. The grand magazine is a large compartment comprising three rooms at the bow that contained the main gunpowder store. In 2005 *Victory's* fore topsail went go on display again after the latest of several conservation programmes. Initially made in the Sail Loft at Chatham in 1803, it is the only surviving sail from the Battle of Trafalgar. Measuring 80ft at its base, 54ft at the head, and 54ft deep, the sail has an area of 3,618 sq.ft. The sail cloth was woven in Dundee and is pockmarked by some ninety shot holes and further apertures, some of which may have been caused by nineteenth century souvenir hunters.

HMS WARRIOR

In the half-century after Trafalgar, technological change altered the face of naval warfare and *Warrior* was probably the most significant ship in that process. Some wooden battleships (First-Rates), similar in appearance to *Victory,* had been modified or built with auxiliary steam propulsion and screw propeller, whilst retaining their full sailing rig. However, their wooden construction made them extremely vulnerable to the new explosive shells which were replacing roundshot. To help overcome this, iron-cladding could be added to the hulls, as in the French *La Gloire.* The Royal Navy's response was the *Warrior,* ordered in 1859, the world's first iron-hulled battleship. She was launched on 29 December 1860 at Blackwall by her builders, the Thames Ironworks. In the coldest winter for fifty years, with frozen snow covering the shipyard, she froze to the slipway. Braziers burned around the ship's sides but extra tugs and hydraulic rams were needed whilst hundreds of men ran from side to side on her upper deck, trying to rock her free. After twenty minutes she finally slid down into the river. After fitting out she commissioned on 1 August 1861 at Portsmouth. She was classified as a steam frigate because she only had one main gundeck, but was later to be reclassified as a battleship.

Warrior's steam engines, built by Penns of Greenwich, were rather inefficient, requiring large amounts of coal, and sixty-six stokers toiled in temperatures of about 43 degrees Centigrade. Coaling up took two days, as teams of seamen and marines filled two cwt (100kg) wicker panniers aboard the collier alongside. The panniers were hauled through the gunports, lifted over the deck and emptied down chutes to stokers in the bunkers below. The ship's sixteen-piece band played to help keep up the morale of the blackened crew. Coal dust also blackened the gun deck and took a week to clean up afterwards. Hence it was not surprising that *Warrior* was the first warship to have fitted washing machines, and she retained a full spread of sail for everyday use. Under sail her telescopic funnels could be lowered and her propeller lifted out of the water to reduce drag.

The central section of the hull was an armoured box or citadel, built of 4.5 inch (11cm) wrought iron plate with 18in teak backing. The protection thus provided to the guns and machinery was vastly superior to that afforded by a wooden hull. The size, speed, construction

HMS *Warrior* seen from the Gosport ferry. (Author)

and firepower of *Warrior* made her the most powerful warship afloat, rendering all her predecessors obsolete. In June 1862, following trials and modifications, she joined the Channel Squadron where her deterrent effect contributed to a decline in the aggressive intentions of the French and she never fired a shot in anger. In 1869 she left her familiar cruising grounds of the Channel and Bay of Biscay, joining her sister-ship *Black Prince* to tow a new floating dock from Madeira to Ireland Island, Bermuda, the base of the West Indies Squadron.

In 1871 she paid off for a major refit at Portsmouth but was to see no further operational service. *Warrior* was recommissioned in 1875 as a ship of the first Reserve, her design by then being obsolescent. At Portland, and then from 1881 on the Clyde, her duties were as a static guardship, drillship for the Royal Naval Reserve, and coastguard headquarters. Every year she was manned by the Reserve for a five or six week summer cruise. These were largely uneventful, although on the first – when *Warrior* was flagship – *Iron Duke* rammed and sank *Vanguard* off the Irish coast. In 1883 *Warrior* was paid off from the Reserve at Portsmouth. Her engines, boilers and guns were removed and for several years she was laid up in Fareham Creek. In 1902 she became the depot ship for destroyers at Portsmouth, flying the flag of the flotilla captain. In 1904 she became part of the naval torpedo school, HMS *Vernon*, joining two wooden steam battleships in Portchester Creek. In 1923 *Vernon* moved ashore at the Gunwharf, and *Warrior* was renamed C77 and moved to Pembroke Dock in 1929 to become a floating oilstore and jetty for refuelling warships, a role that lasted until 1978. Some 5,000 ships refuelled alongside her in the fifty years that she was there. It was a happy accident that because of such unglamorous duties she survived to become a subject for restoration, and was towed to Hartlepool in 1979 to begin this process.

A 110-pounder breech-loading gun on *Warrior*. (Author)

Warrior's hull was basically sound, having been maintained in reasonable condition by the Royal Navy. New bulwarks and much new decking were required. The rest of the ship was in very poor state and almost all of the original equipment and fittings had been removed – only a capstan and two pumps remained. Her top deck was covered in 200 tons of concrete which had to be removed. Replicas of the engines and guns were manufactured, often using modern materials – sheet steel instead of cast or wrought iron in the engines, and fibreglass mouldings for the guns. The rebuilding took eight years, costing £6.5m, and restored the ship to magnificent condition. In June 1987, she returned to her old base, Portsmouth, where the local council had spent £1.5m on a new jetty and supporting facilities for her. Her position near the Hard allows her to be seen to good effect and attracts the attention of visitors and ferry passengers to the Historic Dockyard. At the end of 2004 she was dry-docked at Portsmouth so that her bottom could be repainted.

Facts and Figures

Overall length: 420ft (128m) Beam: 58ft (18m); Draught: 26ft (8m)
Displacement: 9,210 tons
Armour: sides 4.5in over 208ft of the central part of the hull.
Horsepower: 5,287 Speed: 14.5 knots (under steam), 13 knots (under sail).
Main Armament: ten breech-loading 110-pounders, twenty-six muzzle-loading 68-pounders.
Crew: 705 (including 127 Royal Marines) Coal: 850 tons; Sail Area: 4,580 sq.m

Above: A muzzle-loading 68-pounder gun and armoury on *Warrior.* (Author)

Right: The *Warrior's* present day captain with a brass saluting gun. (Author)

Upper deck and ships' boats, HMS *Warrior*. (Author)

The officers' dining room on HMS *Warrior*. (Author)

Warrior's figurehead. (Author)

The wheels and binnacle on HMS *Warrior.* (Author)

The captain's quarters on *Warrior*. (Author)

HMS *Warrior*, broadside. (Author)

HM MONITOR M33

M33 is one of very few warships to survive from the First World War, and can be seen in No.1 dry dock, close to HMS *Victory*. She was built in Belfast by Workman, Clark, under sub-contract from Harland & Wolff, as a monitor designed for coastal bombardment. *M33* was one of the last group in a class of nineteen ships, and was fitted with 6in guns to a design then in production for the secondary armament of the *Queen Elizabeth* class battleships. Her construction in just three months was remarkably rapid, to meet the demands of the Dardanelles campaign in the Eastern Mediterranean – to where she was dispatched on completion in June 1915. She assisted in the Suvla landings in August, and for the remainder of the Gallipoli campaign gave close support off the Suvla beachhead. Following the withdrawal from Gallipoli in January 1916 she moved north to Salonika to support the Allied flanks against the Bulgarians. From mid-1916 to mid-1918 *M33* was part of one or other of the detached squadrons operating in the Aegean, and then returned home to prepare for service in the White Sea.

In 1919 she was recommissioned and sent to North Russia with the British Relief Force, joining four of her sister ships in the Dvina River Flotilla to cover the withdrawal of Allied and White Russian forces after the Revolution. Arriving at Archangel in early June, the force sailed upriver to bombard Bolshevik positions. Throughout the campaign the river depth was unusually low, so in order to return to Archangel at the end of August the guns had to be removed and loaded onto barges. *M33* was fitted with dummy guns made from driftwood, pipes and biscuit tins to fool the enemy. Her guns were reshipped and she undertook one further mission upriver to cover the evacuation of the last British troops. Two of her sister ships ran aground on the way back to Archangel and had to be scuttled. *M33* returned to Chatham in October 1919.

After the war she was converted to a minelayer at Pembroke Dockyard and her guns were removed. In 1924 she was given the name *Minerva* and served as a mine-laying training tender to HMS *Vernon* at Portsmouth. As a minelayer she could carry fifty-two mines. In 1937 she was prepared for sale but was retained and recommissioned at the

The monitor *M33* in No.1 Dock. Behind her can be seen *Invincible* (left) and *Ark Royal*. (Author)

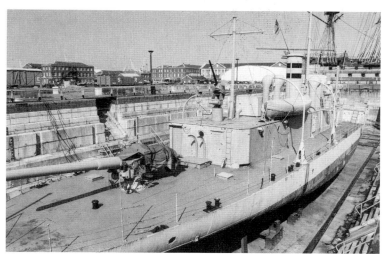

Stern view of *M33*. (Author)

outbreak of war in 1939 as an accommodation ship for naval trawlers at Portsmouth until 1944 when she was reduced to a hulk as a boom defence workshop. Renumbered *C23*, she continued to serve as a hulk in Portsmouth Harbour well into the post-war period. She was eventually taken in hand at Hartlepool in July 1987 for restoration to her original appearance with the assistance of Hampshire County Council.

Facts and Figures

Displacement: 520 tons standard, 580 tons full load.
Length: 177ft/ 54 m Beam: 31ft/9.5 m. Draught: 6ft/1.9 m
Machinery (former): Twin shaft steam reciprocating, 400 IHP, 10 knots.
Armament: Two 6in and one 6-pounder guns.
Range of 6in guns: 14,700 yards at 17 ½ degree elevation.

HMS RAME HEAD

Rame Head is the only Royal Navy ship from the Second World War which still has a role in the service. She is now moored in Fareham Creek and is used for Royal Marines training. Completed in August 1945 at Vancouver, she was one of sixteen maintenance ships built in Canada using standard wartime merchant ship hulls. The class were all named after headlands around the coast of the British Isles. The hold space was used for workshops and *Rame Head*'s role was to act as a mobile repair ship for destroyers and frigates. Because they spent most of their time in harbour, maintenance ships did not have to be fast and were propelled by steam reciprocating engines of modest power.

After commissioning in August 1945 she sailed from Vancouver with her sister ship *Duncansby Head* to join the British Pacific Fleet. *Rame Head* was based at Brisbane, and then Hong Kong and Japan. In February 1946 she became the senior officer's ship for the Captain, Escort Forces, in the British Pacific Fleet, until September of that year when she returned to the U.K. In December 1946 she became a refit accommodation ship at Sheerness, before moving to Devonport in 1957 in a similar role.

Despite her austerity design she has survived through a succession of unglamorous harbour roles. In 1960-1962 she was modernised at Chatham Dockyard, and was in commission for a short time from March 1962 for post-refit trials before being reduced to reserve at Chatham. In October 1963 she moved to Portsmouth as joint headquarters ship for the Senior Officer Reserve Ships, replacing her unmodernised sister *Mull of Galloway* alongside the cruiser *Sheffield*. She was later joined in reserve there by the only other two ships of the class to be similarly modernised – *Berry Head* and *Hartland Point* (though unlike *Rame Head,* both of these saw active service after their modernisation). In June 1966 she was towed to Devonport for a refit, returning to Portsmouth, again under tow, in January 1967. Between 1971 and 1973 *Rame Head* was an accommodation ship at Londonderry, followed by similar use at Portsmouth until December 1984 when she moved to Rosyth as a refit support ship. She returned to Portsmouth in March 1987, and

Rame Head in Fareham Creek. (Author)

from December 1990 was at Portland, returning to Portsmouth in January 1996. She has been periodically dry-docked for survey and the repainting of her underside.

Facts and Figures

Displacement: 8,580 tons (standard) Length: 441ft Beam: 57ft; Draught: 22.5ft.
Armament: now disarmed; previously eleven 40mm anti-aircraft guns (after modernisation)
Machinery: Single shaft, triple expansion steam, 2,500 IHP; Speed: 10 knots
Complement: 445 (after modernisation).
Builder: Burrard Dry Dock, North Vancouver; Launched: 22 November 1944.

STEAM PINNACE 199

This 50ft steam pinnace is a rare survivor from the great naval arms race which preceded the First World War, when Britain vied with Germany to produce more Dreadnoughts, the powerful battleships of that era. *199* is thought to be one of two such pinnaces carried aboard HMS *Monarch*, an *Orion*-class battleship which served in the Royal Navy from 1912 to 1919. *Monarch* had been ordered from Armstrong Whitworth on the Tyne in 1909, a year when the public clamour for more Dreadnoughts to be built was at its height and the catchphrase 'We want eight and we won't wait' was coined by a Tory MP. On commissioning she joined the Second Battle Squadron and took part in the Battle of Jutland.

Steam Pinnace *199* was built in 1911 by J. Samuel White at Cowes and is the only remaining steam pinnace from the 634 such vessels in the Navy at the start of the First World War. As well as serving as ships' boats, pinnaces could be armed to patrol the capital ship anchorage as a defence against torpedo boats. In this role they were often referred to as picket boats, and *199* can now be seen mounting a Hotchkiss 3-pounder gun. This gun was built in 1887 and as late as 1945 was fitted to an armed yacht which was sunk later in that year. The gun was found by a trawler in its nets in 1980.

In 1918 she was converted to an admiral's barge by adding a counter stern and a brass funnel. In 1919 *Monarch* was reduced to reserve at Portsmouth and was sunk as a target in 1925. *199's* movements thereafter are uncertain. She is believed to have been used as a dockyard launch and possibly as a tender to the Military Hospital at Netley on Southampton Water. She was sold in 1949 and in 1952 became a houseboat on the Thames. Her condition deteriorated over the years and she was eventually sold for £5 to an antique dealer for restoration. This failed and in 1979 she was acquired by the Royal Naval Museum at Portsmouth. Her original steam engine and boiler had been removed. A pinnace boiler and contemporary steam engine, a two cylinder compound, were provided by the Royal Navy's engineering school at HMS *Sultan*, and restoration was completed in 1984. A further major overhaul took place between 1999 and 2001 when she emerged in

The steam pinnace *199* at Gunwharf Quays. (Author)

her present shape to take part in the Festival of the Sea. In 2003 her undersize propeller was replaced by one of the correct size.

Steam Pinnace *199* is maintained and operated by volunteers and can be seen steaming in Portsmouth Harbour and the Solent in the summer months, often with her crew in period costume. Her programme includes appearances at a number of events in the area. The Royal Navy Museum also has a Victorian 30ft sailing gig which is kept afloat.

HMS BRISTOL

Bristol is anchored off Whale Island and serves as a Harbour Training Ship for National Cadet Forces and the Royal Navy. Launched in 1969, she was completed in 1972 by Swan Hunter, on the Tyne, and is still in commission as an HM Ship, with a crew of forty-three officers, ratings and civilian staff. She was powered by combined steam and gas turbines, the former venting through her forward funnel and the latter through the twin after funnels.

A Type 82 destroyer, she was the prototype of a class designed to escort a new class of aircraft carriers which, due to defence cuts, were never built. Three planned sister ships of the *Bristol* were also cancelled. She was the largest ship classified as a destroyer to be built for the Royal Navy, though the Type 45's now under construction will be bigger. *Bristol's* completion allowed her to act as a trials ship for her new weapon systems, which occupied the first three years of her career. During early trials her steam plant failed and for many months she operated on gas turbines alone. She was refitted between 1976 and 1978 when the steam plant was repaired and two 20mm anti-aircraft guns were fitted. Her first operational commission commenced in 1980 when she became flagship of the Third Flotilla. Equipped to act as a Flagship and Command and Control headquarters for a Task Group, she served as such in the later stages of the Falkland Conflict in 1982. Although listed for withdrawal in the 1981 Defence Review, she was reprieved by the Falklands conflict. Leaving Portsmouth on 10 May 1982, she led the first reinforcement group which included the destroyer *Cardiff*, the frigates *Active*, *Avenger*, *Andromeda*, *Minerva* and *Penelope*, and the RFA's *Olna* and *Tidespring*. They joined the Carrier Battle Group off the Falklands on the night of 25/26 May, by which time the Falklands had been recaptured. On 1 July *Bristol* took over from *Invincible* as flagship of the Task Force, until being relieved in this role by *Illustrious* on 27 August. *Bristol* arrived back at Portsmouth on 17 September and at the end of 1982 entered Portsmouth Dockyard for a short refit when two 30mm guns were added. She was at sea again in 1983 spending short spells overseas before being taken in hand at Portsmouth for a major refit. Her now-obsolete Ikara anti-submarine missile system was removed, and she suffered a severe boiler room explosion that injured three men. In 1987 she was fitted with a deckhouse to accommodate 100 cadets and replaced the County Class destroyer *Fife* as Flagship of the Dartmouth Training Squadron, offering sea training for officer cadets. *Bristol* paid off in 1991 and her armament of guided missile systems and guns was removed, allowing her to take up her current role in 1993, replacing the County Class destroyer *Kent*.

Built to a very high standard, her wide passageways and roomy mess decks are ideal for the large number of trainees who pass through her every year. The mess decks (dormitories) and cabins can sleep about 460 and in a typical year (2001) over 5,000 RN personnel and 12,000 youths were trained aboard her.

Facts and Figures

Length: 507ft (154m) Beam: 55ft (16.5m) Draught: 17ft (5m)

Displacement: 6,300 tons Original Complement: 407 (twenty-nine officers and 378 ratings)

Propulsion: Two AEI steam turbines in tandem with two Rolls-Royce Olympus gas turbines, producing a combined maximum of 74,600shp, twin screws. Speed: 30 knots Range: 5,000 miles at 18 knots.

Original Armament: One twin Sea Dart anti-aircraft missile launcher, one Ikara anti-submarine homing torpedo launcher, one 4.5in gun, one Limbo anti-submarine mortar; two 20mm and two 30mm guns were later added.

HMS *Bristol* off Whale Island. (Author)

HMS *Bristol* arriving at Portsmouth following her service in the Falklands. (Dave Page Collection)

HM SUBMARINE HOLLAND 1

The Royal Navy's first submarines were the five Holland class, named after their inventor, John Holland. He was an Irishman who emigrated to the United States where, following the production of a number of experimental craft, he sold his *Holland VI* to the United States Navy in 1900. This boat was generally thought to have been the first truly successful submarine after three hundred years of experimentation by various inventors. The Royal Navy had been sceptical of submarines – regarding them as the underhand weapons of weaker powers. However, in 1901 they decided to assess them more fully and, in the absence of a British design, ordered five Holland boats which were built under licence by Vickers at Barrow-in-Furness at a cost of £35,000 each.

Holland 1 was launched as the Navy's first submarine on 2 October 1901 and completed in February 1903 (though three of her sisters entered service before her). She had a length of 63ft 10in and a surface displacement of 110 tons. Her engines were petrol (for surface use) giving a speed of 7.5 knots, and electric (for use when submerged) giving a submerged speed of 7 knots. The sixty battery cells which fed the electric motor were located under the internal deck. She was armed with one 18in bow torpedo tube and carried two reloads. With a crew of eight she had a range of 236 miles, or twenty miles submerged at 7 knots. Her hull's uncluttered teardrop shape contributed to the high underwater speed and endurance. The design also allowed the submarine to dive, surface and change depth at an angle, using hydroplanes to pitch the bow up or down (Holland's competitors usually aimed to keep their craft level at all times). This, together with the power available, gave her high maneuverability underwater. She was designed to dive to a depth of 100ft, but it is unlikely that this depth was achieved and normally she would not dive below 50ft. This was sufficient since the threats of sonar detection and depth charges were not yet present.

Given that the boats had only 4ft of freeboard, the hatch had to be kept closed in any sea other than a flat calm. When on the surface this made the watchkeeper's position on the nearly flat top of the Holland's exposed casing perilous. The solution, fitted only to

Holland 1's torpedo tube. (Author)

Holland 2, was to raise the upper hatch by constructing a higher conning tower, which became a common design feature of later submarine classes. Conditions inside the hull were extremely cramped and primitive, though the lack of internal bulkheads made best use of the space. Unlike Holland's earlier boats though, the design incorporated a basic periscope.

The Hollands were used for trials and training, thus enabling the development of the submarine classes that were to serve in the First World War. These larger and slightly better-equipped boats soon entered service with the Royal Navy, whilst two of the Hollands were lost in accidents. Then, in 1913, *Holland 1* was sold but sank under tow near the Eddystone en route to a breakers yard in Wales. In 1981 the minehunter HMS *Bossington* located the wreck and a year later she was salvaged to become a museum exhibit. Despite anti-corrosion treatment she rusted badly on display. In 1994 the Submarine Museum built a huge glassfibre tank and submerged the hull in 800,000 litres of sodium carbonate. Soaking the submarine in this way removed the chloride ions that were the cause of the uncontrollable corrosion and in 1998 she emerged to be displayed in a new gallery with a powerful dehumidification system. Visitors can now go aboard to explore the interior of the boat. Although many important pieces of equipment would have been removed before her final voyage to the breakers yard she still has intact the main components – engine, motor, propeller shaft, ballast tanks and torpedo tube. Her hull betrays the evidence of sixty-nine years of corrosion and decay on the seabed.

HMS ALLIANCE

The sixteen A Class submarines were designed in the Second World War for the war in the Pacific but were completed too late to see action. Larger than the preceding classes, they were faster on the surface and had a greater range – and, also to suit the Pacific conditions, they had an air-conditioned compartment.

They had an all welded hull which was prefabricated in sections and welded together on the ways. *Alliance* was built by Vickers-Armstrong at Barrow and completed in May 1947. Later that year she undertook a record dive, staying submerged for thirty days and covering 3,193 miles between Gibraltar and Freetown, Sierra Leone. This was accomplished with the use of her snort – a tube which drew air into the hull from the surface, allowing the use of her diesel engines.

The snort was developed from the *schnorkel* that had been fitted to German U-boats. One of the A Class, *Affray*, left Gosport on 16 April 1951 with seventy-five men aboard and reported at 2115 that she was diving south of the Isle of Wight, but was not heard from again. Two months later she was found lying in forty-three fathoms of water, thirty-seven miles south of St Catherine's Lighthouse. After salvage, it was discovered that her snort tube had fractured, leaving a 10in hole in her pressure hull, but the cause of the fracture was not discovered.

Originally *Alliance* was fitted with ten torpedo tubes, a 4in gun forward of the conning tower and a 20mm gun on the rear end of the conning tower. When she was modernised in the late 1950s, the guns were removed and the number of torpedo tubes was reduced to six. Her appearance was greatly changed – the hull was streamlined, a larger streamlined conning tower was constructed of aluminium, and a large sonar dome was fitted above the bow. She finally paid off at Gosport in 1973 and was subsequently used as a static harbour training ship at HMS *Dolphin,* replacing *Tabard*, until December 1976 when she was herself replaced by *Grampus*. In 1978 an appeal was launched for her preservation and in 1979 she was placed on blocks to become the centre-piece of the Royal Naval Submarine Museum at Gosport. On 24 August 1981 she was opened to the public. Her main significance is

Alliance on display
at Gosport.
(Author)

as the sole surviving RN submarine (apart from midget submarines) of Second World
War design, albeit incorporating post-war modifications. The last opportunity to preserve
a British submarine in original war-time condition had been lost in 1967 when *Tally-Ho*
(which had an impressive war record) left Portsmouth for the breakers.

Facts and Figures

Displacement: 1,120 tons standard, 1,385 tons full load (surface), 1,620 tons submerged.
Length: 283ft Beam: 22.25ft. Draught: 17ft.
Machinery: Two shafts, Vickers-Armstrong 8-cylinder supercharged diesel engines, 4,320
    BHP giving a surface speed of 19 knots. English Electric electric motors, 1,250 SHP,
    giving a submerged speed of 8 knots.
Range: 10,500 nautical miles surfaced. 16 nautical miles at 8 knots, or 90 nautical miles
    at 3 knots fully submerged.
Armament: Six 21in torpedo tubes.
Complement: 60 to 68.

Service History

During the era of *Alliance's* service, the Royal Navy maintained a world-wide submarine
presence, with squadrons in Malta, Halifax (Canada), Sydney (Australia) and Singapore,
as well as at the home bases of Gosport, Devonport and Rothesay (later Faslane). *Alliance*
served in five of these locations. Her first commission was with the Third Submarine
Flotilla at Rothesay. During this commission she completed her epic underwater trial
in the tropical waters between the Canary Isles, off which she submerged on 9 October
1947, and Sierra Leone, surfacing off Freetown on 8 November. She was paid off in
December 1948 to refit at Chatham and recommissioned in September 1949, joining the

Alliance, alongside a 4in gun, the last to be carried by a British submarine (HMS *Andrew),* at the Royal Naval Submarine Museum. (Author)

Second Submarine Flotilla at Gosport. She was based at Gosport for the next seven years, from July 1951 being part of the 5th Submarine Flotilla (which was renamed the Fifth Submarine Squadron in January 1952). This period included three refits at Portsmouth.

On 5 September 1956, she left Gosport to join the Sixth Submarine Squadron at Halifax, Nova Scotia, replacing *Ambush,* and served there until February 1958. *Alliance* arrived home at Gosport on 5 March 1958 – rejoining the Fifth Submarine Squadron for three months before entering reserve at Gosport in June. In September 1958 she was taken in hand at Devonport for her major refit and modernisation. She was recommissioned in April 1960 for the Third Submarine Squadron at Faslane, transferring to the Second Submarine Squadron at Devonport seven months later. In February 1962 she started a twelve month refit at Chatham, returning to Gosport in February 1963 as part of the First Submarine Squadron based there.

This stay at Gosport was short, for she left on 28 May 1963 for Singapore, via the Cape of Good Hope, to join the Seventh Submarine Division – arriving there on 10 October. This was an active period of confrontation with Indonesia to prevent incursions into Malaysia, and RN forces in Singapore were considerably augmented. In 1965 she was used to test a new camouflage paint scheme in the Far East. *Alliance* left Singapore on 9 June 1965, having been replaced by *Oberon,* and arrived at Devonport on 15 July. There she was taken in hand for a refit which was completed in August 1966, when she rejoined the First Submarine Squadron at Gosport for a full commission. On 12 January 1968 she went aground off Bembridge, Isle of Wight, at 8 p.m. She was refloated thirty-six hours later by tugs and salvage vessels, and was undamaged. In February 1969 she entered Chatham Dockyard for her final refit, emerging in April 1970 to join the Second Submarine Division at Devonport. In 1971 she was damaged by a battery explosion whilst alongside at Portland. Her final service was in NATO exercises in the North Atlantic and Mediterranean in January – February 1973 before paying off at Gosport on 5 March. From November 1973 until December 1976 she was the static harbour training submarine at Gosport.

HMS *Alliance* leaving Gosport, where she was part of the First Submarine Squadron, January 1967. (Author)

HMS *Alcide,* an A-class submarine photographed in 1947, showing the original appearance of this class. (Dave Page Collection)

HM SUBMARINE X24

X24 is a Second World War midget submarine which carried out two successful operations on the Norwegian coast. The X-craft were designed to penetrate protected harbours in order to place limpet mines against the hulls of enemy vessels. In one of the most famous exploits *X6* and *X7* inflicted heavy damage to the German battleship *Tirpitz* in a fjord in Northern Norway. *X24* was in action in April 1944 when she was towed by the submarine *Sceptre* to attack the Lakesvaag floating dock at Bergen. This dock was regularly used by U-boats and was thought capable of taking the crippled *Tirpitz*. The operation was brilliantly conducted, but instead of sinking the floating dock *X24* sank the freighter *Bahrenfels* which was lying nearby. The operation was repeated in September 1944 and this time *X24* totally destroyed the floating dock.

X24 was 51ft (16m) long with a surface displacement of 27 tons (30 tons submerged). Her surface speed of about 6 knots reduced to 4½ when submerged, powered like *Alliance* and other conventional submarines by diesel and electric engines. The Gardner diesels were of the type which powered London buses. Although cramped and uncomfortable, these boats were quite sophisticated, with most of the features found in normal-sized submarines. Like some others of the class, *X24* was built inland by a precision engineering firm with no experience of shipbuilding, in her case Marshalls (the traction engine builders) in Gainsborough.

For operations X-craft were manned by a passage crew and towed to the vicinity of their target area by a larger submarine. For most of the passage the X-craft remained submerged, only surfacing to ventilate the boat at regular intervals. Then – when approaching the vicinity of the target – the operational crew, consisting of the Captain, First Lieutenant, Engineer and Diver would take over. The craft had a wet and dry chamber allowing for the egress and recovery of the diver to clear or cut through obstructions (e.g. defensive nets) and attach limpet mines to the side of the enemy vessel. The boats also had large, curved side charges (bombs with time fuses) attached to their hulls that could be released from inside the hull to be set under the target ship's hull. Each

Biber 105 in the Weapons Gallery at the Submarine Museum, showing a torpedo fitted to the side of her hull. (Author)

charge contained two tons of explosive. The craft then withdrew to rejoin the mother submarine. Many X-craft crews received decorations for gallantry, including four Victoria Crosses – but losses were high.

Now at the Submarine Museum, *X24* is the only X-craft on display anywhere that saw operational service in the Second World War. In 2004 she was renovated for exhibition as the centrepiece of the new Fieldhouse Building at the museum.

Biber 105

This German Second World War midget submarine is also on display in the Submarine Museum. She was one of many similar one-man submarines built in 1944 to attack the Allied D-Day invasion forces. They could be carried on lorry trailers to their launching sites on French beaches but only three craft actually made it to Normandy before D-Day, and the others were then based at Rotterdam from where they made raids into the North Sea. Their range was 100 miles on the surface or eight miles submerged. However, very few craft actually returned from their missions: often they were destroyed by aircraft attack or simply foundered after losing their direction. Their design was inadequate and the crews were poorly trained. Another of the 324-strong class, *Biber 90*, is on display at the Imperial War Museum. She was discovered with her dead operator drifting off the North Foreland by the minesweeper HMS *Ready* in December 1944, and was later tested extensively by the Royal Navy. Presumably *Biber 105* was also recovered by the Royal Navy and she is said to have spent some time on display at HMS *Ganges*, the boy seamen training establishment at Shotley near Ipswich, before coming to Gosport.

Each boat was armed with two 21in torpedoes which were fitted to the sides of the hull. They were propelled by petrol and electric motors and could dive to a depth of 100ft. In 2003, *Biber 105* was restored to pristine working condition, with the replacement of many parts, by apprentices at Fleet Support Ltd in Portsmouth Dockyard, featuring in the Channel Four television programme 'Salvage Squad'. The 9m long boat undertook a test dive in No.8 Dock at the Naval Base before being moved to the museum's weapons gallery.

THE ROUND AND SQUARE TOWERS

At the narrowest part of the harbour entrance, the Round Tower provides excellent close up views of ships entering and leaving Portsmouth Harbour. In 1415, King Henry V sailed from the harbour in his ship *La Trinitee* for France, after planning his campaign at Portchester Castle. His accompanying fleet had embarked an army of 50,000 men at Southampton and Portsmouth. Henry's conquests in France were confirmed at the Battle of Agincourt. In recognition of the strategic importance of Portsmouth, he authorised the building of the Round Tower. It was constructed in *c.*1416-22, mainly of wood, whilst opposite it, on the Gosport side, a wooden tower was built in *c.*1426 (where Fort Blockhouse was later sited). The Round Tower was reconstructed entirely of stone in about 1494. These two towers were known as the 'king's towers' and between them a heavy, defensive, iron chain was laid which could be raised and lowered by capstans: at the foot of the Round Tower is Capstan Square where such equipment was installed. Similar chains and booms were used across the harbour mouth up until the Second World War. Adjacent to Capstan Square is Tower House which was the home and studio of the marine artist William L. Wyllie, who moved there in 1906.

In 1494 work also began on the Square Tower and the associated bulwarks, to the seaward side of the Round Tower. The Square Tower was initially used as a gun platform and an artillery powder magazine, and later as a water and meat store. In the nineteenth century it was used by the Admiralty to mount a semaphore tower. On the south-east side of the Square Tower is the Saluting Platform, originally built by the Tudors to carry bronze and iron guns which defended the harbour entrance.

The ramparts seen today between the Round and Square towers were part of a major rebuilding of the defences ordered by Charles II and carried out in the 1680s by Sir Bernard de Gomme, a Dutch military engineer. They were further rebuilt in 1848-50. Within them, adjacent to the Square Tower, is the Sally Port, an opening in the wall which gave access to the seaward side, providing one of the main embarkation points for ships that were anchored at Spithead. It now gives access to Victoria Pier, originally built in

The Round Tower
from Broad Street.
(Author)

The Square Tower.
(Author)

1842 to serve the steam ferries which crossed to the Isle of Wight and France. The present
pier dates from about 1930. There is a second sally port nearer the Round Tower, giving
access to the beach.

Between the Round Tower and Broad Street is the arched wall which was part of
Point Barracks. These barracks were built between 1847 and 1850 and accommodated the
artillerymen who manned the 18-gun battery between the two towers.

The Round and Square Towers were early parts of what over four centuries became
very extensive fortifications to Portsmouth, extending on the seaward side from the
Needles Channel to the four sea forts built at the eastern entrance to the Solent – Spit
Sand, Horse Sand, No Man's Land, and St Helens Forts. On the landward side a chain of
forts was built between Stokes Bay and Portsdown Hill.

THE CAMBER AND POINT

The Camber is Portsmouth's ancient commercial port and is situated in Old Portsmouth. It was developed in the twelfth century by a wealthy Norman wool merchant and shipowner, Jean de Gisors, who also gave land nearby to build the chapel which was to become the chancel of Portsmouth's Anglican cathedral. Although it was overshadowed by the greater naval activity in the harbour, Portsmouth's mercantile shipping has a long and interesting history, and of course the naval and military activities of Portsmouth provided a large market for the incoming seaborne trade.

The Camber imported some of the first potatoes and tobacco into England in 1586 after the colonizing of Virginia by Sir Walter Raleigh. Catherine of Braganza arrived in Old Portsmouth from Portugal in 1662, and brought tea to Britain for the first time. At this time Portsmouth was not an important commercial port, but in the late seventeenth, and eighteenth centuries its trade grew significantly. By the early eighteenth century there was a thriving coastal trade. From Sussex, Southampton, the Isle of Wight, the West Country and Wales the cargoes included farm produce, malt, timber, cattle, wine, brandy and bottles. The trade in coal from the North-east and Wales grew in importance, and was to become a very significant import by the nineteenth century. Locally there were many hoys sailing to the various parts of the harbour and to the Isle of Wight. Salt from the various Hampshire harbours and estuaries was exported, but was also imported at times. Fish came from both local fisheries and further afield, such as Hastings and Brixham, as well as cod from Newfoundland. All these incoming supplies were both for the town and for the dockyard and other service establishments such as Haslar Hospital and Royal Clarence Yard.

There was considerable foreign trade in the seventeenth and eighteenth centuries. As well as cod, the New World and the West Indies supplied skins, whale oil, tobacco, timber, fruit and sugar. From the Iberian Peninsula and France came wines and other produce, at least when the respective countries were at peace. From the Baltic and Russia came pitch, tar, hemp and timber. The expanding British Empire led to the port being used by the ships of the East India Company, the Levant Company (serving the eastern

The Camber, with Portsmouth Cathedral in the background. (Author)

Mediterranean) and the Royal African Company. The East India Company traded with, and had extensive interests in India, China and the Far East. Passengers, their servants, and officials left from Portsmouth, having come down from London by coach and wagon. Because of the constant wars with Holland, France and Spain the ships often sailed in convoys with naval escorts, and were themselves armed. The East India Company had its own army and detachments embarked at Portsmouth for India. The Company had ship repair facilities and storehouses at Portsmouth, and at least one East Indiaman was built at Gosport. In 1767, when Lord Clive arrived at Portsmouth from India on the *Britannia* the ship's cargo included raw silk, redwood and saltpetre. In 1787 the first group of convicts set sail from here for Botany Bay in Australia.

Until well into the twentieth century the Camber, and also the quays at Flathouse, still had a busy traffic of coasters trading with the Channel Islands, the Isle of Wight, other British ports and the near continent. In 1963 the port handled about a million tons of merchant shipping. The imports were bricks, coal, government stores, timber, oil fuel, fruit, vegetables and general goods. Exports included scrap iron, cars, government stores, chemicals and general goods. At the Camber there were eight berths, a total quayage of 1,825ft and 18ft of water at high tide. A regular weekly service to Amsterdam was operated by the Holland Steamship Company. At Flathouse, where most of the imports were timber, there were five berths, a total quayage of 1,100ft and 18ft 6in of water at high tide. Colliers serviced the gas works at Flathouse, the power station at the entrance to the Camber, and the Camber yard of Corralls (formerly Fraser and White) which had storage space for 15,000 tons of coal. All this coastal trade declined in the 1970s when lorries and containers took much of the business – some of it transferring to the roll-on/roll-off

Above: Quebec House. (Author)

Right: The former Dutch Consulate, now the clubhouse for Portsmouth Sailing Club. (Author)

ferries which berthed at the new Ferry Port at Flathouse. There were also two thriving ship and yacht building yards in the Camber. The most important of these was Vosper which became famous for the motor torpedo boats and motor gun boats developed in the 1930s and built in large numbers during the Second World War. The other yard, Harry Feltham, was a successful yacht builder. The sites of these two yards have now been re-developed as residential housing. Now the Camber mainly hosts fishing boats and pilot launches.

Point is the promontory at the end of Broad Street, and was landscaped in 2000 to take better advantage of its superb vista over the harbour and its entrance. The area was once notorious for its numerous pubs and ale-houses and was frequented by the notorious Press Gangs who enlisted unwilling men into the Navy. On the wall of the Bridge Tavern is a mural based on Thomas Rowlandson's painting 'Portsmouth Point' which conveys the raucous atmosphere of the day. The floating bridge vehicle ferry from Gosport landed at Point until its closure in 1959. In Tower Street buildings of interest include Tower House, which was home to the marine painter William L. Wyllie (1851-1931), and the weather-boarded Quebec House (1754), a former salt-water bathing house with four bathing rooms which filled with the tide. The house was renamed to commemorate the landing at Point of the body of General Wolfe, victor of the Battle of Quebec in 1759. Opposite Quebec House is the former Dutch Consulate, now the headquarters of Portsmouth Sailing Club. In the seventeenth century ships of the Dutch East India Company called at Portsmouth and the Dutch consul doubled as the company's agent.

W.L. WYLLIE

William Lionel Wyllie was one of Britain's foremost marine painters and in the twenty five years that he lived in Tower House, Old Portsmouth, he produced countless paintings and etchings of the local maritime scene, as well as historical studies such as his panorama of the Battle of Trafalgar which now hangs in the Royal Naval Museum close to the *Victory*.

He was born in 1851, the son of the London painter William Morrison Wyllie, who had five children – all of whom drew and painted. Summers were spent at their house at Cap Gris-Nez, near Boulogne, and were to influence William Lionel's interest in the sea and everything connected with it. Amongst other things he sketched the wrecks of ships that met their end on the rocky coastline there. He and his brothers were all strong swimmers and braved a fierce gale to carry a rope to help rescue the crew of a sinking schooner in 1869. At the age of twelve he was accepted as an art student at Heatherley's in London and at fifteen was enrolled at the Royal Academy School where he was to study under Millais and Landseer amongst others. Two years later an oil, 'Dover Castle and Town', was accepted for the Royal Academy summer exhibition.

In 1871, he and his brothers converted an old ship's boat into a yacht in which they sailed the French and Belgian coasts, giving William the first hand experience which was to inform the technical aspects of his paintings. In this and other yachts he also sailed the length and breadth of the Thames and Medway, painting and sketching the teeming naval and merchant shipping as he went. In 1885 he moved with his wife Marion and their three sons to Hoo Lodge overlooking the Medway at Rochester. This was also the year when his acclaimed pen and ink 'Toil, Glitter, Grime and Wealth on a Flowing Tide' was bought for the Tate Gallery, enhancing his status and leading to other commissions. By 1906, when he moved to Portsmouth, he had five sons and two daughters, and in the following year was elected to the Royal Academy. He converted the 'Yacht Chambers, Stores and Wharf' into an impressive residence but left one store untouched to provide a meeting place for the Sea Scouts troop which he founded in 1907 at the behest of Lord Baden Powell. Wyllie was fascinated by the scene at Point and after the First World

Tower House and the Round Tower. (Author)

War added the tower to his house so that he could see out over the Solent above the Round Tower. In 1912 another Portsmouth resident, Fred T. Jane (of *Jane's Fighting Ships* fame) produced *The British Battle Fleet*, containing thirty-seven coloured plates by Wyllie. During the war Mr Balfour, the First Lord of the Admiralty, gave permission for him to cruise in ships of the Grand Fleet in the North Sea and he made hundreds of studies of the Navy at sea. It is an indication of his prolific output over sixty years that the National Maritime Museum has over 5,000 of his paintings and etchings in its collection.

Wyllie helped set up the Society for Nautical Research in 1910, and chaired the foundation meeting which lobbied successfully for the preservation of HMS *Victory*, one of his favourite subjects. In 1920 he was one of the principal founders of Portsmouth Sailing Club, which is still housed in the former Dutch Consulate building at Point. His last series of watercolours, 'The Old Portsmouth and the New Southsea', was produced shortly before his death at the age of eighty in 1931. His greatest work, 'The Panorama of the Battle of Trafalgar', was a huge oil painting on a canvas measuring 42ft by 12ft, and was started in 1929 and took nine months intensive work – in which 'WL' was assisted by his daughter Aileen. Remarkably, at the time of the painting's completion, Wyllie was aged seventy-nine. The Panorama was painted on a curved framework in a specially-built annexe to the Victory Museum and turnstiles were installed, allowing people to watch Wyllie at work for the fee of two old pence. The new attraction was opened by King George V in July 1930. In 1999, following restoration and re-hanging, the picture was re-opened to the public as the centre-piece of a Trafalgar Experience exhibition in a new Victory Gallery in the Royal Naval Museum in the dockyard.

HMS *Sirius*, the Leander-Class frigate, passing the Round Tower. (Author)

Wyllie died in April 1931. In recognition of his tireless efforts in the fundraising campaign for the original restoration of HMS *Victory,* and his contribution as the leading British marine painter of his generation, Wyllie was accorded full naval honours at his funeral. After the service at Portsmouth Cathedral his coffin was taken from Point in the stern of a cutter from the battleship *Nelson,* rowed by Sea Scouts of his own troop, to an admiral's barge lying off. This took him to Portchester Castle where he is buried at St Mary's Church. As the barge passed the *Nelson, Victory* and *Warspite* they dipped their ensigns in a mark of respect. The entire front and back cover of the *Daily Mail* was given over to his funeral. Sir Hugh Casson wrote of Wyllie's ship paintings, 'He never ceased to draw them in every size and shape and in all weathers. He drew them as a seaman would…with deep practical understanding.'

FORT BLOCKHOUSE AND HMS DOLPHIN

For ninety years Fort Blockhouse was home to the Royal Navy's submarine service. However, the spit of land on which it stands had been of strategic importance to the defence of Portsmouth Harbour for centuries before that, lying as it does on the Gosport side of the narrow harbour entrance. Shortly after the Round Tower was completed on the Portsmouth side a wooden tower was erected on the Gosport side, in about 1426. These were the 'king's towers' from which a 'mighty chain of iron' was laid across the harbour mouth. This could be raised by capstans and floats to prevent enemy vessels entering the harbour.

In 1495 a blockhouse (a building that could block an enemy attack) was built on the site to house five guns. This was strengthened in Henry VIII's reign, in 1539, and re-armed in 1667 when a nineteen or twenty gun battery was installed by Sir Bernard de Gomme for Charles II. However, the original fortifications had by then decayed and the point was poorly protected. A new fort was built in the early eighteenth century, incorporating De Gomme's south-east facing battery of guns. This seaward battery, which is clearly visible from the Round Tower, was by 1825 converted into a casemented battery with thirteen embrasures. It is, in origin, the oldest part of the fort. The south-west side dates from the new fort of about 1708, whilst at this time the north-west and north-east sides were wooden palisades. Finally, major improvements were proposed in 1845, the two wooden walls were replaced with brick walls and accommodation buildings and by 1863 Fort Blockhouse was essentially in its final state. The north bastion and parts of the perimeter walls are still in tact but much is obscured by more modern buildings.

The Royal Engineers came to occupy the fort from about 1873 as a base for sea-mine warfare. By 1904, the Army considered the fort obsolete and it was handed over to the Navy, to become the first submarine base, commissioning in May 1905. Its appropriate name, HMS *Dolphin*, was taken from an old sloop – one of two hulks which provided accommodation afloat for the base. Soon the base expanded beyond the fort and was used to support both operational submarines and submariner training. In peace and war the

The submarine *Thermopylae* approaching HMS *Dolphin* in April 1967. (Author)

jetties of *Dolphin* in Haslar Creek were usually lined with submarines. By 1994 though the last submarines had gone, as defence cuts left only nuclear-powered boats in the Navy, and these were based at Devonport and Faslane.

In late 1997, the Submarine School was moved to HMS *Raleigh* at Torpoint in Cornwall, and *Dolphin* paid off on 30 September 1998. With *Dolphin* closed, only the Submarine Escape Training Tank survived, being considered too expensive to move. This 100ft tower holding 20,000 gallons of water had been completed in 1954 and allows submariners to simulate escape from a stricken submarine. The *Dolphin* site was taken over by the tri-service Royal Defence Medical College (which itself subsequently closed in 2002) and 33 Field Hospital.

HMS Hornet

At the foot of Haslar Bridge, on the Haslar side, a coastal motor boat (CMB) base was established in the First World War by the Navy and in 1926 was named HMS *Hornet*. CMB's were fast streamlined boats carrying torpedoes, which were superseded in the 1930s by motor torpedo boats (MTB). *Hornet* closed in 1934, but was recommissioned in December 1939 following the outbreak of war. In the Second World War, many MTBs were based at *Hornet* as well as motor gun boats and motor launches. There were repair workshops and slipways at the base, and Haslar Gunboat Yard, situated on the Alverstoke side of Haslar Creek, was used for refitting the boats. This yard had twenty covered sheds in a continuous line facing the creek, served by two slipways and a steam transporter, designed by Isambard Kingdom Brunel, to move the boats laterally from the slipways to the sheds. The yard was opened in 1857 for the repair of the steam gunboats used in the Crimean War, and was not closed until 1978.

The Portsmouth-built submarine *Token* leaving Gosport in April 1967. This photo shows her after being streamlined and modernized in the 1950s, and can be compared with the photograph of her sister *Tireless* before modernization (page 32). Also visible is the submarine Escape Training Tank tower. (Author)

Built by Vosper, ,the fast petrol boat *Gay Archer* was completed in 1952 and served at HMS *Hornet*, but had a short operational life because of the decision to axe coastal forces. She was placed in reserve at Hythe on Southampton Water before being sold in 1963 for conversion to a yacht. She has survived and is now being restored to her original apperance. (Dave Page Collection)

MTB 538 was a prototype Vosper boat with a new hull shape. She was renumbered MTB1601 then FBD1601. A Vosper advertisement from 1949.

Hornet was decommissioned in September 1957 by when the Royal Navy's coastal forces had been effectively disbanded and the few remaining fast patrol boats moved to HMS *Dolphin*. Part of the site was taken over by the Hornet Sailing Club whose members were serving or retired members of the Royal Navy. In 1972 the Joint Services Sailing Club was also established there for training and recreational use by the three services. It was renamed the Joint Services Adventurous Sail Training Centre in 1991. Part of the site was given over to the Submarine Museum in 1980.

A War Memorial to the small ships of the Coastal Forces lost during the Second World War is looked over by the Hornet Sailing Club clubhouse. The names of the Coastal Forces bases are inscribed on the memorial. The clubhouse is the original wooden Wardroom and Captain's quarters of HMS *Hornet*.

ROYAL CLARENCE YARD

If, at its peak, Portsmouth Dockyard was the largest industrial complex in the world, Gosport could claim to have one of the earliest large-scale food-processing factories, at Royal Clarence Yard. The yard was opened in 1828, replacing facilities in Portsmouth, to meet the demands of the expanded navy and help overcome the reputation for corruption and inefficiency which the Navy's victualling service had acquired.

The site at Weevil Lane, which possessed a brewery and cooperage, associated with a well to provide water for brewing, was purchased by the Navy in the mid-eighteenth century. The creek was deepened and new wharves were built. In 1827 the decision was taken to move other victualling operations there, and a bakehouse, mill, slaughterhouse, storehouses, offices, and steam engines to power the equipment were built. The yard also distributed clothing, bedding and utensils. In the 1840s a railway line was built, connecting to the London & South Western Railway, before Portsmouth itself was connected. A station was built in the yard to which Queen Victoria travelled and then boarded her yacht for Osborne House on the Isle of Wight. The wharves were also busy with barges and small steam lighters which distributed provisions to the fleet.

The sailor's daily ration of one pound of ship's biscuit, eight pints of beer, plus meat, butter, cheese, peas and oatmeal was supplied by Clarence Yard to Portsmouth-based ships. Cattle arrived at the yard either through the gates on the hoof from local markets or by ship to be landed by steam crane, and were herded into pens before being slaughtered, butchered, salted and barrelled at the yard. The Salt Meat Store was one of a number of buildings destroyed in air raids in 1941. One of the original buildings which still survives is the large granary on the quayside which fed the bakehouses. The biscuit, or hard tack, was produced and double baked on a mass production system devised by Thomas Grant, who was Storekeeper from 1831 to 1850. His production lines could produce 10,000 biscuits an hour. In 1838 nearly eleven million pounds of biscuit was baked at the yard. By the time they were consumed aboard ship the biscuits were often infected with weevil, a small insect. Around the start of the twentieth century warships were equipped to bake

The Superintendent's House (left) and the Porter's Residence, built in 1830, at Royal Clarence Yard. (Author)

The granary on the quayside at Royal Clarence Yard, undergoing conversion in 2004 for residential use. (Author)

The main gate at Royal Clarence Yard. (Author)

fresh bread, and in 1907 biscuit production ceased at Clarence Yard. Grant also developed a distilling machine to convert salt water to drinking water on ships. Rum was blended and barrelled at the yard, superseding beer aboard ships, until 1970 when the Navy's rum ration ended.

The yard was closed in April 1995 and was sold for residential development. The adjacent Forton Fuel Depot which had supplied coal, and later oil, to the fleet remained open and Royal Fleet Auxiliary tankers continued to visit the Oil Jetty.

1 The aircraft carriers *Ark Royal* (left) and *Invincible* berthed at Portsmouth. (Author)

2 The Type 42 destroyer *Liverpool*. (Dave Page Collection)

3 The Type 23 frigate *Norfolk* at Devonport. (Dave Page Collection)

4 The mine countermeasures vessel *Cattistock* leaving Portsmouth. The Hampshire Rose on her funnel indicates that she is part of the Portsmouth mine countermeasures squadron. (Author)

5   HMS *Dasher* at Portsmouth. (Author)

6   HMS *Invincible.* (Dave Page Collection)

7 HMS *Victory* as painted by W.L. Wylie in 1928. (Portsmouth City Museums)

8 Brittany Ferries *Val de Loire*. (Brittany Ferries)

9 Brittany Ferries *Normandie.* (Brittany Ferries)

10 Brittany Ferries *Bretagne* at St Malo following a crossing from Portsmouth. She transferred to the Plymouth-Roscoff route in 2005. (Brittany Ferries)

11 Condor Ferries *Commodore Goodwill*. (Author)

12 Admiralty House. (Author)

13 The Steam Factory and No.2 Basin, with visiting yachts, at the International Festival of the Sea in 1998. (Author)

14 The converted lightship *Mary Mouse 2* at Haslar Marina. (Author)

15 P & O's *Pride of Bilbao* passing through the harbour entrance. (Author)

16 The Wightlink ferry *St Faith* entering Portsmouth Harbour. (Author)

17 The fast ferry *Caen Express* entering Portsmouth harbour. She was withdrawn from the Portsmouth–Caen service at the end of 2004. (Author)

18 HMS *Warrior*. (Author)

19 The paddle steamer *Waverley* leaving Portsmouth. (Author)

20 *Matthew*, the replica of John Cabot's caravel, seen in No.5 Dock at the 2001 Festival. Behind her is the Georgian building (1802) which housed the block mills of Marc Isambard Brunel. (Author)

21 The Brazilian ship *Cisne Branco* in the Tidal Basin at the 2001 International Festival of the Sea. (Author)

22 The Italian barquentine *Palinuro* at the 2001 International Festival of the Sea. (Author)

23 The Norwegian barque *Christian Radich* entering Portsmouth harbour for the 2001 Festival. (Author)

24 The Mexican barque *Cuauhtemoc* at the South Railway Jetty, IFOS 2001. (Author)

25 The Polish ship *Dar Mlodziezy* arriving at Portsmouth for IFOS 2001. (Author)

26 The assault ship *Intrepid* in No.3 Basin at IFOS 1998. (Author)

27 The Batch 3 Type 42 destroyer *York* alongside at Portsmouth. (Author)

28 The tug *Bustler* at Portsmouth. (Author)

29 The tug *Helen* entering Portsmouth Harbour. (Author)

30 The three Hunt class at IFOS 1998, left to right *Berkeley*, *Ledbury* and *Hurworth*. (Author)

31 The RAF air-sea rescue launch *102* at IFOS 1998. She was built by the British Power Boat Company at Hythe in 1936, and is now based at the Military Powerboat Trust site at Marchwood, also on Southampton Water. (Author)

HASLAR HOSPITAL

Medical provision for sick and injured sailors was poor in the seventeenth century, and their 'sick lodgings' were often in ale-houses and hovels. Many of the sick died or deserted, and diseases originating on overseas service were sometimes spread to the local population. The idea of a naval hospital at Portsmouth was put forward in 1653 but it was not until 1744 that the proposal was finally accepted and two years later work began on the site acquired at Haslar Farm. The development preceded construction of the large Georgian brick buildings in the Dockyard (other than the Royal Naval Academy).

Before 1795 very few naval buildings were designed by professional architects, instead plans were drawn up by the dockyard's master shipwright and submitted to the Navy Board's surveyor in London. Because of its size and specialization Haslar Hospital was an exception and Theodore Jacobsen was employed as the architect. Typically for the Georgian period, the design was an ambitious one, with four wings of three storeys around an open quadrangle. The first wing opened in 1753 followed by two further wings in 1760. In 1762 the Hospital Church of St Luke was opened, but the fourth wing was never built. Even so, the hospital was the largest brick building in Europe, and by the end of the eighteenth century nearly 2,000 patients could be treated in the eighty-four wards. Patients were usually brought by boat to a jetty in Blockhouse Lake, and it was not until 1795 that the first bridge was built over Haslar Creek – connecting the hospital to the town of Gosport. The hospital was surrounded by high walls and iron railings to prevent the escape of patients who had been press-ganged into the Navy.

From the Napoleonic wars through to the Falklands conflict the hospital at Haslar has treated sick sailors. In the American War of Independence and the Peninsular Wars it also treated prisoners of war and soldiers. Now a tri-service establishment, the Royal Hospital Haslar provides care for both the military and local communities, in partnership with Portsmouth NHS Trust.

Haslar Hospital – the main building (1753). (Author)

The Canada Block at Haslar Hospital (1917). (Author)

PRIDDY'S HARD

Priddy's Hard was the navy's arsenal, storing, manufacturing and repairing all sorts of ammunition and explosives. It was named after Jane Priddy from whom land was purchased in 1750 to extend Gosport's fortifications with the building of Priddy's Hard Fort. In 1767 citizens of Portsmouth petitioned for the removal of the gunpowder magazine at the Square Tower in Old Portsmouth, following an explosion there. It was decided to move it to Priddy's Hard and the new Powder Magazine was completed in about 1771, although it was not fully operational until 1777. This building survives as one of a number which now house the Explosion museum.

In the second half of the nineteenth century there were many developments in naval armaments including large calibre guns, shells using new types of explosive, mines, and torpedoes. Over thirty new buildings were erected to cope with these new munitions and the increased volume of work. The stores for cordite and gunpowder were surrounded by earthworks to limit damage in the event of an accident. Further growth occurred in the First World War when Priddy's Hard was responsible for the filling and repair of cartridges and shells and the storage of ammunition. The site was expanded to eighty acres and fifty-five additional storehouses, laboratories and workshops were built. Additional armament depots were also built nearby at Bedenham, Frater and Elson before and during the war. These were connected by a standard gauge railway linked to the main Gosport -Fareham line. Priddy's Hard had three piers and a Camber Basin which allowed for the seaborne transportation of munitions to the depot and its distribution from there on lighters to the fleet in Portsmouth Harbour or at Spithead.

After the First World War the naval functions of Portsmouth's Gunwharf, including small arms, were transferred to Priddy's Hard. In the mid-1930s the depot employed 1,344 staff. This expanded rapidly during the Second World War when over 1,700 women were employed and by 1944 the total workforce was 3,700, to meet the massive requirements of the D-Day Landings. The women worked twelve hour days in the manufacture and repair of armaments and the associated packing cases: 20,000 tons of ammunition and

The Powder Magazine (1771) at Priddy's Hard. On the right is a 4.7in gun of the type fitted to Second World War destroyers of the S, T, V and W Classes.

50,000 rockets were prepared for the invading forces. After the war there was a gradual run-down in activities culminating in the closure of the depot in 1989 and much of the land was then sold for residential development.

The Explosion Museum, sited in the original Powder Magazine, features naval armaments from gunpowder to the guided missile and nuclear weapon age. It was funded with £3.5m from the Millennium Commission under the Renaissance of Portsmouth Harbour Millenium Scheme, allowing the development of Gosport's waterfront from Haslar to Priddy's Hard. A new attraction for 2005 is a gallery studying the victualling operations of the nearby Royal Clarence Yard, showing how food was prepared and stored for the Navy in the nineteenth century. There will also be a three-quarter view full scale model of a transport hoy, a reproduction of the Foreman's Office, and the quayside along which the boat will be moored. Access is also being made to a Victorian explosives vault.

VOSPER THORNYCROFT

When the tug *Hercules* slid down the ways in the Camber in 1889, at a time when Britain built more ships than any other country, no-one would have thought that her builders would outlive most of the other British ship builders to become one of the very few survivors of a once huge industry. That Vosper managed to survive and prosper was due to the drive and versatility of the founder – Herbert Edward Vosper, and the abilities of Commander Peter Du Cane, managing director from 1931 to 1963, who on two occasions transformed the company and its products. Under Du Cane, design innovation became the company's greatest strength and paved the way for the merger in 1966 with the Southampton ship builder John I. Thornycroft, opening up the capacity to build larger ships.

Herbert Vosper was himself an innovative engineer. In 1870, at the age of nineteen or twenty, he patented a valve linkage for a steam engine. The following year he began setting up workshops on the Camber for refitting and repairing coastal vessels. He soon diversified into the design and production of a range of marine steam engines for small craft. The works was an impressively integrated one, with ferrous and non-ferrous foundries, machine, boiler and fitting shops, a smithery, and woodworking shops. As well as building steam engines, Vosper was a pioneer in the internal combustion engine, both oil and paraffin fired. The company also made boilers and pumps, and a range of patent anchors. In the 1880s Vosper moved into the building of small ships and launches, with iron, steel or wooden hulls. They were very varied in size and type, from dinghies and lifeboats to yachts and tugs of 70-80ft, and were mainly powered by Vosper's own steam and oil engines. The *Hercules*, built for Shoreham Harbour Trustees, was one of the first.

Vosper continued to head the firm until his retirement in 1919. The 1920s were lean years where reliance returned to refit work, including the virtual rebuilding of Scott's *Discovery* for a further Antarctic expedition. In 1931 the decision was made by Peter Du Cane, who had just joined the firm, to concentrate on fast craft. His arrival had been preceded by a leading designer of hydroplanes and fast craft, Fred Cooper, who was

MTB 22 was built by Vosper in 1939. (Dave Page Collection)

recruited in 1930. At this time the company was, rather incongruously, owned by Fraser and White – the Portsmouth coal merchants, but Du Cane and a business partner took a controlling interest. The fast picket boat *Advance,* designed by Cooper, was the first of the new line but soon afterwards Du Cane took over design and all other aspects of the business. He concentrated on hard-chine wooden planing hulls and, as well as bespoke designs, a number of standard hulls were built in large numbers – such as the jolly boats, picket boats, and admiral's barges built for the Royal Navy. They were powered by Vosper V8 marine petrol engines, based on the contemporary Ford engine. The largest of the boats were 45ft picket boats built to replace the steam pinnaces like *199* (which has been restored at Portsmouth) aboard battleships. These developments led in 1939 to the design and building by Vosper of a new 40ft royal barge for the Royal Yacht *Victoria and Albert.* Another large order in the 1930s, from the Air Ministry, was for refuelling tenders for seaplanes. The company also designed and built *Bluebird II* for Sir Malcolm Campbell, which took the world water speed record at 123 knots in 1939.

By 1936, with the increasing prospect of war, the Royal Navy was again investing tentatively in coastal forces and a number of motor torpedo boats (MTB) were built by the British Power Boat Company at Hythe on Southampton Water. Vosper responded by building as a speculative venture an experimental MTB of 68ft length, which, before being armed, achieved 48 knots on trials. Once fully armed and loaded she achieved 44 knots, and proved her seaworthiness in winds of Force 7. This led to her being purchased by the Admiralty as *MTB 102*, and was the start of the extensive programme of MTB development and construction by Vosper during the Second World War. The Admiralty ordered some seventy-five Vosper 70 or 71ft MTB's in 1939 and 1940. To cope with the demand a new yard was opened at Portchester in 1940, and even then some of the craft had to be subcontracted to other boatyards around the country. A further sixteen were ordered in 1942, followed in 1943 and 1944 by about twenty-eight of the slightly larger and improved 73ft type. Also of 73ft were the fifteen RAF air-sea rescue launches of 1941-42.

After the war, orders were sparse, but included several experimental craft for the Admiralty. The first of these was *MTB 1601*, completed in 1948, which was the prototype of a revised hull form with a higher chine at the bow, the forward sections more deeply vee-d and a fuller deckline. This became the standard hull form in the late 1950s and was used for two decades, most notably on the Royal Navy's *Brave* Class. The steam gunboat *Grey Goose* was re-engined by Vosper, installing Rolls Royce gas turbines which had been developed at the end of the war for aircraft. A prototype fast patrol boat (FPB) HMS *Bold Pathfinder* was built with combined gas turbines and diesel propulsion, the Mercedes-Benz diesel engines being taken from surrendered German E-boats. A variety of other craft were built but the company's financial position was parlous. Then came the Korean War which prompted the Admiralty to order new fast patrol boats based largely on wartime MTB designs as an interim measure. Vosper's bacon was saved by the order for four of the *Gay* Class, and this was followed by fifteen air-sea rescue launches for the RAF, and four *Dark* Class diesel-engined FPBs. Then came the very successful gas turbine *Brave* Class of FPB – of which only two were built because the Royal Navy had decided to abandon coastal forces. This could have spelt disaster for Vosper, but the firm decided to set up a sales organization (at that time a rare thing for shipbuilders) and seek orders abroad, and to bring in modern management methods to ensure that contracts ran smoothly

Vosper's Camber yard in April 1967 showing two gas turbine fast patrol boats (on slip and left) and two diesel patrol boats under construction. (Author)

and showed a profit. Another speculative venture, the FPB *Ferocity,* was built in 1959 as a slightly smaller and modified version of the *Braves.* Orders followed from Germany, Denmark, Malaysia, Brunei and Libya, and sixteen boats were built in the 1960s plus three *Scimitar* class for the Royal Navy in 1970 for training purposes. Simultaneously, a slower, steel-hulled, diesel-engined patrol boat was designed for developing countries, leading to large orders from Malaysia and elsewhere. From this developed larger corvettes of up to 200ft in length for African navies. These were a tight fit in the Camber yard, and it was timely therefore that in 1966 a merger was agreed with John I. Thornycroft of Woolston, Southampton. The new company secured an order to design the Royal Navy's new Type 21 frigate, three of which were built at Southampton. Thornycroft had been building ships there for the Navy since 1907, and went on to build three of the Type 42 destroyers.

Thus the 1960s established Vosper Thornycroft as an international warship builder and that has continued to this day. Frigates have been built for Brazil, Iran and Libya, corvettes for Oman, and fast attack craft for Egypt, Oman, Qatar, and Kenya. The company pioneered the use of fibre reinforced plastic in large hulls, firstly in the minehunter HMS *Wilton.* This led to the construction by Vosper Thornycroft of most ships of the *Hunt* and *Sandown* classes of minehunters. Meanwhile, also for the Royal Navy, vessels have been built in the *Archer* and *Tyne* Classes.

The Portchester yard continues to operate, whilst the Camber (Broad Street) yard has been closed for redevelopment of the site. In 2003 a new shipbuilding facility was opened by the VT Group (as the company is now known) within Portsmouth Dockyard, replacing its Woolston yard which launched its last vessel (the yacht *Mirabella V*) in January 2004. In the same month work started on building the modules for the Type 45 destroyers at Portsmouth. The facility contains two new large enclosed building sheds. The biggest of these is the Ship Assembly Hall, of 130m length, which builds complete ships or large modules of ships. These are constructed from sub-units fabricated in the Unit Construction Hall which is situated alongside the Ship Assembly Hall. Nearby is the Steelwork Production Hall which was converted from an existing dockyard building to supply the required steelwork sections and panels to the two construction halls. The first vessel to be built at the new Portsmouth facility was the barge *Woolston,* of 1,350 tonnes, which will be used to transport the VT-built bow sections, masts and funnels of the Type 45's to the BAE shipyard on the Clyde. She was named and rolled out of the main ship assembly hall on 21 June 2004.

The VT Group has a joint venture company with BAE Systems, Fleet Support Ltd, which operates the refitting and repair operations of Portsmouth Dockyard. In 2004 VT won a contract to operate the naval dockyard at Auckland, New Zealand, and has also diversified into many other public sector contracting activities.

Restored MTBs

Two of the Vosper MTBs have been restored by the British Military Powerboat Trust, based at Marchwood on Southampton Water, and can occasionally be seen at Portsmouth. One of these is *MTB 102,* the original Vosper prototype of 1937 (see photo, p.115). After purchase by the Admiralty she saw active service in 1939 and 1940, mainly in the Channel,

HMS *Sabre* was a fast training craft, modelled on a fast patrol boat, built by Vosper in 1970. She was sold in 1986. (Dave Page Collection)

and, during the Dunkirk evacuation of the British Expeditionary Force, she crossed the Channel eight times. When the destroyer *Keith* was bombed by a Stuka dive bomber, Rear-Admiral Wake-Walker transferred to *MTB 102,* using her as his flagship for the last two nights of the operation directing the incoming and outgoing vessels at Dunkirk from the bridge. A Rear-Admiral's flag was improvised from a dishcloth and red paint, and *MTB 102* was the third to last vessel to leave the scene.

Originally she was fitted with a single torpedo tube in her bow, but following trials this was replaced with two 21in tubes on the sidedecks at a 10 degree angle to the centreline. She also carried a 20mm gun or two 0.5in machine guns. By 1943 she was obsolete as an MTB and was transferred to the Army and named *Vimy*. In 1944 she carried Winston Churchill and General Eisenhower on their review of the ships assembled on the south coast in preparation for the D-Day landings. At the end of the war she was sold to become a motor cruiser on the east coast. Then, in 1973 whilst under conversion to a houseboat, she was acquired by the Sea Scouts at Lowestoft and converted into a static headquarters ship. Luckily, she was to find a role in the 1976 film *The Eagle has Landed* for which she underwent restoration to full seagoing state. The hull and decks received further repairs and reinforcement in 1983 and 1990. She has been re-engined four times, the latest being in 2002, in each case with diesel engines, though originally she had Italian petrol engines by Isotta Fraschini. She has been seen at Portsmouth at the Festivals of the Sea and on other ceremonial occasions.

MTB 102's original success led Vosper to gain orders for MTB's from Romania, Greece, Norway and Sweden, though with the outbreak of war most of the craft under construction were requisitioned by the Admiralty. They included *MTB 71*, a 60ft boat that had been ordered by the Royal Norwegian Navy. She was armed with two 18in torpedoes and four machine guns. She also had Isotta Fraschini engines, with a top speed of 39 knots. Commissioned in July 1940, she joined the Eleventh MTB Flotilla at HMS *Wasp* in Dover. Two months later, during a heavy air attack on Dover, she was damaged, including a fire in her wheelhouse, and repairs at Whitstable took four months. In June 1941 she was slightly damaged in action with enemy escort vessels off Etaples and her Petty Officer Stoker was killed. The next month, in further action off Berck buoy, she was holed below the waterline and was out of action for two months whilst under repair on the Thames. In November 1941, she re-commissioned with a Royal Norwegian Navy crew and joined the First MTB Flotilla at HMS *Beehive* in Felixstowe, and had a skirmish with E-boats off Kwinte Bank. In February 1942 she reverted to an RN crew and was involved in the Dover Straits, searching for the German *Scharnhorst*, *Gneisenau* and *Prinz Eugen* during their daring Channel dash on 12 February. *MTB 71* was recorded as being damaged that day by shellfire and was then under repair at Brightlingsea for six months. In September 1942 she transferred to the Fourth MTB Flotilla at Felixstowe and was in action off the Hook of Holland two months later. In June 1943 she paid off, and like *MTB 102,* was transferred to the Army. She was laid up by the RASC at Portsmouth and cannibalized for spares for her sister ship *MTB 72* which had also been taken over by the Army. Then, in September 1944, she was returned to the Navy at HMS *Hornet*, and sold the following year for use as a houseboat at Birdham. Her owner, Mr Pudney, died in 1992 and she was acquired by Hampshire County Council in conjunction with the MTB 71 Group Charitable Trust. She underwent partial restoration within Portsmouth Dockyard and was on display at the 1998 Festival of the Sea. She was then moved to Marchwood for further restoration as a static exhibit.

MTB 71 at the 1998 International Festival of the Sea. (Author)

R. V. Triton. (Author)

R. V. Triton

In 1998 VT was commissioned by the Ministry of Defence to design and build a research vessel (RV) to explore the potential of the trimaran hull form in naval and military applications. *Triton* is of all steel construction and was completed in August 2000, the fast building cycle being achieved using modular construction techniques. She is operated by QinetiQ (formerly DERA) and based at Portsmouth. The trimaran hull has inherently good seakeeping and performance, and gives advantages of reduced costs, reduced radar signature, increased length giving greater stability, and more area for the upper deck which could be used for the flight deck and hangars for helicopters and for extra armament. A Lynx helicopter has successfully carried out a series of landings and take-offs from the deck of the *Triton*. VT has developed designs for trimaran frigates and patrol craft and feasibility studies by the MoD may lead to a larger version of this hull form being used for the replacement for Type 23 frigate.

Facts and Figures

Displacement: 1,100 tonnes Length: 98.7m Beam: 22.5m Draught: 3.2m

Propulsion: 2 x Paxman diesels, 3.5 MW, plus auxiliary electric propulsors, 350 KW.

Speed: 20 knots (8 knots when using the auxiliary engines). Range: 3,000 nautical miles.

Complement: twelve plus twelve scientific personnel.

CAMPER & NICHOLSONS

Fort Charles, a small fort built by Sir Bernard de Gomme in 1679 on the foreshore of Gosport became the site of the world famous yacht and shipbuilders Camper & Nicholsons. It is still the company's main site though today nothing of the fort remains. By 1778, the lease of the abandoned fort had passed to a brewer who used it as an ale-house before building the Castle Tavern (which still stands outside the yacht building yard). It then passed to Francis Amos, a shipwright indentured in London, who is thought to have arrived in Gosport in 1782. He established a small shipwright's business at Beach Street (facing the entrance to Haslar Creek, where tower blocks now stand) and in 1792 took over the lease of the Fort Charles site. He is thought to have built small, open wherries for use by the harbour watermen, and later progressed to building small trading vessels such as the smack Commerce (12 tons) of 1821 and yachts such as the cutter *Whim* (14 tons) of 1822.

In 1809 he was joined by his great-nephew William Camper as an apprentice. Camper, like Amos, came from the East End of London where his family had been shipwrights for over one hundred years. When Amos died in 1824 Camper took over the lease of the yard and set up in his own name. He built strong links with wealthy members of the newly established Royal Yacht Squadron and was able to position the firm in the emergent yacht building industry. He launched the cutter *Breeze* (41 tons) in 1836 and her victory that year in the King's Cup helped Camper establish himself as a builder of fast yachts over the next twenty years. In 1842 the fourteen-year-old Ben Nicholson joined the yard as an apprentice. He had been raised on a convict hulk in the harbour – on which his father was overseer. His was a most successful appointment, for by 1855 he was responsible for most of the yard's design work, as well as for its management. The schooner *Aline* (216 tons) of 1860, a very successful racing yacht, was the first genuinely original response to the loss of morale that had followed the defeat in 1851 of British yachts by the America in the first of what became the America's Cup races.

The topsoil schooner *Hoshi* was buit by Camper & Nicholsons in 1908. For about fifty years she was operated by the Island Cruising Club at Salcombe. (Island Cruising Club)

Just before his death in 1863, William Camper handed the business over to Ben Nicholson who began expanding the yard – now called Camper & Nicholson – to double its previous size. He erected the first building shed, joiners shops and sawmill and developed the laying-up yard in Little Beach Street for yacht repair. As well as Nicholson's schooners, cutters and yawls, yachts were built to the designs of leading independent designers such as William Fife and George L. Watson. Nicholson lived at Stanley House, on Stokes Bay, and had three sons – who took over the business to run it jointly after the death of their father in 1906. The second son, Charles E. Nicholson, had emerged as the natural successor to his father through outstanding designs such as *Coquette* in 1891 and it was on his designs that the future of the business was secured. The firm had become a limited company and changed its name to Camper & Nicholsons in 1895 to recognize the participation of the sons. In 1912 the yard of J.G. Fay at Northam, Southampton, was acquired and was later to concentrate particularly on the building and refitting of motor yachts. From 1906, when his *Nyria* was launched, Charles E. Nicholson was recognized as one of the two leading British yacht designers (the other being the older William Fife). Such was the racing success of Nicholson's designs that he secured an order from Sir Thomas Lipton for the 1914 America's Cup challenger, *Shamrock I*. Because the First World War intervened the match was not held until 1920, when *Shamrock IV* was unsuccessful, though she won two of the five races. During the First World War Camper & Nicholsons built coastal motor boats (an early form of the motor torpedo boat) for the Royal Navy and high speed launches, as well as setting up the Gosport Aircraft Company to build flying boat hulls.

The late 1920s and 1930s were the heyday of the company as Charles E. Nicholson's designs reached their zenith. It built the four British J Class yachts (three of which were America's Cup challengers), three 23-metres, the three-masted *Creole* and a dozen 12-metres,

The minesweeper HMS *Stubbington* was built by Camper and Nicholsons in 1956. She was broken up in 1989. (Mark Teadham)

as well as becoming the leading motor yacht builders (with twenty such vessels completed in this period). The J Class had towering masts and high aspect ratio sails with a sail area of 7,500 sq.ft. They were enormously expensive to run and did not compete again after the Second World War (though the C&N-built *Endeavour*, *Velsheda* and *Shamrock V* have since been restored). A third generation of Nicholsons joined the firm, including Charles A. Nicholson who became a successful yacht designer in the years after the Second World War.

During the Second World War the yard turned again to naval construction, building motor torpedo boats (MTBs), motor gun boats (MGBs), motor minesweepers, landing craft and other small vessels. One class of MTBs (*MTB 511-518*) was designed, as well as built, by C&N and boats of this class were retained after the war to operate until the mid-1950s from HMS *Hornet* in Haslar Creek. After the war, yacht-building resumed at the Gosport yard but and was augmented in the 1950s by five Ton Class minesweepers (including the *Stubbington*) of mahogany construction, three Ham Class inshore minesweepers and three Gosport ferries. Thereafter the firm concentrated mainly on yacht building and maintenance, moving into GRP construction. These production yachts ranged from 26ft to 58ft and were built in large numbers, reviving the company's fortunes. In 1981, financial restructuring ended the link with the Nicholson family, and the firm moved away from building production yachts to return to the building and refitting of large luxury yachts such as *Cyrano de Bergerac*, a 127ft ketch of 1993 and *Our Blue Dream*, a 121ft sloop of 1999. The cyclical nature of such work, affected as it was by the fluctuating fortunes of the wealthy and variations to the taxation regime, meant that an independent long term future was difficult to secure. In 2000 the company was acquired by Cammell Laird, but the Gosport yard was sold the following year to Nautor's Swan, a Finnish yacht building company, and continues to focus on yacht and small craft construction, restoration and repair. There has also been refit work on the Navy's *Archer* Class patrol boats. It is a remarkable story of business longevity that Camper & Nicholsons has remained on the same site for 200 years, and has been one of the world's leading yacht builders for the past 170 years.

THE INTERNATIONAL FESTIVAL OF THE SEA

Amongst the most exciting maritime experiences at Portsmouth have been the successive International Festivals of the Sea, staged there in 1998, 2001 and 2005. Huge crowds are attracted to see an impressive array of tall ships, British and foreign warships, classic yachts and numerous other exhibits.

Britain's first International Festival of the Sea was held at Bristol in 1996, with the *Matthew* replica as a centrepiece – her construction was inspired by the 500th anniversary of John Cabot's voyage to Newfoundland in 1497. The next Festival was in 1998 at Portsmouth Dockyard, and drew crowds totalling around 250,000. This was ten times the attendance at the most recent Navy Days at Portsmouth, convincing the naval authorities of the value of the event. The tall ships present included the Russian *Sedov*, *Kruzenshtern* and *Mir*, the Polish *Iskra*, the Argentinian *Libertad* and the replicas *Grand Turk* and *Matthew*. Amongst the warships, which were berthed separately from the tall ships, were *Invincible*, *Fearless*, *Birmingham*, *Liverpool*, *Manchester*, *Nottingham*, *Iron Duke* and *Marlborough*. Access to most areas of the dockyard was possible – giving a rare opportunity to see both historic buildings and modern facilities.

The success of the event led to an even larger Festival in 2001, when nearly 1,000 ships and boats attended, manned by around 15,000 sailors. It was the largest public event of the year in Britain, and the largest maritime event in Europe. Tall ships and warships were intermixed along the jetties. The line up of tall ships was especially impressive, including the Norwegian *Christian Radich*, *Sorlandet* and *Statsraad Lehmkuhl*, the Russian *Sedov*, *Mir*, and *Shtandart*, the Polish *Dar Mlodziezy*, *Iskra* and *Pogoria*, the Italian *Palinuro*, the Brazilian *Cisne Branco,* the Mexican *Cuauhtemoc*, and the British *Prince William*, *Royalist* and *Matthew*. Amongst the warships were *Illustrious*, *Nottingham*, *Exeter*, *York*, *Southampton*, *Grafton*, *Richmond*, *Westminster*, and *Endurance* plus eight foreign ships including USS *Winston Churchill* and the French *De Grasse*.

The next Festival, in 2003, was held at Edinburgh, but the event returns to Portsmouth in 2005 as part of the bi-centennial Trafalgar anniversary.

The German submarine *U26* passes the Argentinian ship *Libertad* at the South Railway Jetty, 1998 Festival of the Sea. *Libertad* was completed in 1963 as a training ship for the Argentine Navy. (Author)

Seen here in the Tidal Basin at Portsmouth for the 1998 Festival of the Sea, the Russian barque *Sedov* is the largest sailing ship in the world. She was built as the German *Magdelene Vinnen* at Kiel in 1921 to carry grain from Australia to Europe. At the end of the Second World War she was ceded to Russia and is now a training ship. (Author)

The Belgian frigate *Wandelarr* is escorted by the tug *Bustler* into Portsmouth Harbour for the 1998 Festival of the Sea. (Author)

Left: Mexican sailors pose for a photographer on the yardarms of the *Cuauhtemoc* at the 2001 Festival of the Sea. (Author)

Below: Left to right, the four white hulled tall ships are *Sorlandet*, *Statsraad Lehmkul*, *Cuauhtemoc*, and *Dar Mlodziezy*, at the 2001 Festival of the Sea. Alongside *Cuauhtemoc* is *Prince William* whilst *Royalist* passes her. (Author)

Above: Two restored coastal forces
vessels, the harbour defence motor
launch *ML 1387* and the Vosper-
built motor torpedo boat *MTB 102*
are seen here in No.3 Basin at the
2001 Festival. Behind them is HMS
Nottingham. (Author)

Right: The Russian ship *Shtandart* at
the 2001 International Festival of the
Sea. (Author)

WHALE ISLAND

Nelson's victory at Trafalgar had been achieved with close range engagement of the enemy, but in the American War of Independence the gunnery of the Royal Navy was less impressive. At this time each ship still employed the methods that its captain considered best, there being no approved system or training. The Admiralty Board was eventually persuaded to create a gunnery school and in 1830 this was commissioned aboard the *Excellent* which was moored in 'ordinary' (reserve) off the north-west corner of Portsmouth Dockyard. Classes were arranged for both officers and men, firing out towards Fareham Creek with targets and range markers set up on the mudflats. The *Excellent* had been built in 1787 as a 74-gun Third Rate ship, and was commanded by Collingwood at the Battle of Cape St Vincent. In 1834 she was replaced by the 104-gun First Rate *Boyne,* a sister ship of the *Victory,* and she in turn was replaced by the First Rate *Queen Charlotte* in 1859 – both assuming the name *Excellent* during their tenure in the gunnery school.

When the Great Extension to the Dockyard was excavated in the late 1860s and the 1870s, thousands of tons of mud was dumped on two dry mudbanks in Portsmouth Harbour called Big and Little Waley, a special railway and viaduct being constructed for its transportation. The new island so formed was used by the gunnery school for musketry drill and firing, there being no other place more suitable. Because it was largely made of mud it was known as Mud Island and was a dreary place, no attempt having been made to dump the mud evenly. Some buildings were erected, still surrounded by mud, to become the first shore training establishment in the Navy. In 1885, a more ambitious plan to develop the island was supported and pushed forward by the then Captain of HMS *Excellent,* Jacky Fisher, the future First Sea Lord who was later to champion the building of Dreadnoughts. As in the original excavation and dumping, convicts were used to drain and level the soil, making roads, extending the railway round the northern perimeter of the island, and in all sorts of work as builders, carpenters and blacksmiths. Barracks, classrooms, drill sheds and sports and leisure facilities were built. In 1891 the old *Excellent*

Seen off Whale
island in 1955 is the
Royal Yacht *Britannia*.
Behind her are ships of
the Reserve Fleet, the
nearest two being the
cruisers *Liverpool* and
Mauritius.

was paid off and the gunnery school became fully established on Whale Island as it became known. Batteries of guns were installed on the island for firing training, and guns of all types were installed in the sheds for training in operating and maintaining them. From 1894 until 1957 a variety of sea-going warships were attached to *Excellent* for firing at sea (including battleships from 1907 to 1939) the last of these being the destroyer *Vigo*. In the late 1950s training in guided missile handling was introduced with the Seaslug.

In 1985, the gunnery school closed and its roles were absorbed by HMS *Nelson,* the Royal Naval Barracks at Portsmouth, and the Royal Naval School of Weapon Engineering at HMS *Collingwood* at Fareham. *Excellent* was reopened in 1994 as a training and administrative establishment for a variety of Royal Navy, Royal Marine and Sea Cadet functions including damage repair and firefighting training, and the national Sea Cadet training centre. The Royal Naval Reserve training centre, HMS *King Alfred,* is also situated on the island. HMS *Bristol,* which has its own commanding officer, is administered from *Excellent* and is connected by a gangway to the island. In April 2002, *Excellent* also became the home of the new Fleet Headquarters, flying the flag of the Commander-in-Chief Fleet, following its transfer from Northwood on the outskirts of London. A new headquarters building was opened in October 2004.

T.S. ROYALIST

Each week twenty-four members of the Sea Cadet Corps, aged between 13½ and 18, set sail in the training ship *Royalist* to undertake training at sea around the coast of the United Kingdom and the near Continent. Based in Haslar Creek, the ship has a permanent crew of six and also carries three adult volunteers. The Captain and the Sailing Master are both Merchant Navy officers. Designed by Colin Mudie and constructed by Groves & Guttridge in Cowes, Isle of Wight, the *Royalist* was completed in 1971. She is operated by the Sea Cadet Association and provides about 800 berths a year. The cadet crew is divided into four watches and each 'learns the ropes' on deck and aloft in his or her part of the ship.

Royalist is a brig and her square-rigged sails total 435 square metres on aluminium masts that are 23m high. Her maximum designed speed under sail is 12 knots. Built of steel, she has twin diesel engines which give her a speed of nine knots in smooth water. The ship is well equipped with central heating and a high standard of safety, navigational and communication equipment. Even so, she provides a challenging environment in which teamwork and personal development can be promoted.

Royalist entering Portsmouth Harbour in August 2001 to attend the International Festival of the Sea. (Author)

THE GOSPORT FERRY

The short crossing between Portsmouth and Gosport is taken by nearly three million passengers a year. Even this figure pales when compared with the over eight million carried each year in the first half of the twentieth century – with large numbers of dockyard and naval personnel commuting from Gosport to work in Portsmouth. This need dated back to Tudor times when the new dockyard's expanding workforce was partly drawn from Gosport, and a regular ferry service was operational from early in the sixteenth century.

Those early ferries were rowing boats (or wherries), which continued to be used until well into the nineteenth century. In 1840 the introduction of a steam powered 'floating bridge' transformed the service. The vessel's two steam engines drove heavy oak cogs which engaged on iron chains laid across the harbour. Steam launches followed in the late 1860s, operated by the watermen who had owned the wherries. When the floating bridge service closed in 1959 there were still eight launches in service, five being steam-powered and three diesel-powered. They were owned by two separate companies, which merged in 1962 and adopted the apple green livery that is still used. The launches were replaced in 1966 by the *Gosport Queen* and *Portsmouth Queen,* built by Thornycroft at Woolston. The two new ferries were quite different to the launches, having a covered main deck which was laid out to allow simultaneous embarkation and disembarkation, and a passenger capacity of 500. Their rotating propeller units fore and aft give them great manoeuverability. In 1971 *Gay Enterprise* (later renamed *Solent Enterprise*) was added for excursion and relief ferry work.

Although the future of the service is now threatened by plans for a tunnel carrying fast rapid transit trams, the Portsmouth Harbour Ferry Company decided in 2000 to build a new ferry, *Spirit of Gosport,* which could supplement or replace the ageing *Queens*. In 2005 another new vessel, *Spirit of Portsmouth,* joined the fleet for excursion work, replacing *Solent Enterprise.*

An early twentieth-century view of steam ferries arriving at the Portsmouth terminal. Behind, a train is passing over the viaduct towards the South Railway Jetty. (Valentine's)

Portsmouth Queen (like her sister ship *Gosport Queen*) has an open upper deck which gives good views over the harbour, and a covered main deck. (Author)

Spirit of Gosport was completed in 2001 and has a general layout which is similar to the Queens. She has a capacity of 300 passengers and is seen here at the Portsea terminal. (Author)

Vadne, a steam ferry built by Vosper in 1939, rots on the foreshore of Forton Lake. In the Second World War she was requisitioned for war duties in the Examination Service, spending some of her time at Freetown in West Africa. In 1959 she was badly holed in collision with the frigate *Redpole*. Withdrawn in the nineteen-sixties, a project to use her as a yacht club headquarters collapsed, as did a restoration attempt. Two of the diesel launches, *Vita* and *Ferry Queen*, survive as excursion boats on the Thames. (Author)

THE ISLE OF WIGHT FERRY

The most frequent traffic in and out of Portsmouth Harbour is that of the Isle of Wight ferries operated by Wightlink. Fast passenger ferries run from Portsmouth Harbour Station to Ryde Pier, whilst car ferries ply between the Gunwharf Road terminal and Fishbourne. The best vantage point to view these ships is at Point in Old Portsmouth.

The earliest recorded ferry service from the Isle of Wight fishing village of 'Ride' to Portsmouth was set up in 1420 by the Lord of the Manor in Ashey. In the 1600s local fisherman were required to provide a service, and failure to do so resulted in a fine. In 1796 the first purpose-built ferry entered regular service: *The Packet* was a large sailing boat which made the crossing twice a day. The first steamship service commenced in 1817 with *Britannia,* and in 1880 the railway companies serving Portsmouth took over the service, a situation that prevailed until 1984.

For many years paddle steamers dominated the route, with the last (*Ryde*) paying off in 1969. The last of the traditional diesel ferries, *Southsea,* made her final crossing in 1988. The replacements were high speed catamarans, *Our Lady Patricia* and *Our Lady Pamela.* With a speed of 29½ knots, they can cross in fifteen minutes. In 1999, the yellow and white striped 'FastCat' livery was adopted, and further capacity was added in 2000 when the larger *Fastcat Shanklin* and *Fastcat Ryde* entered service.

The need for a vehicle ferry led in the early 1900s to steam tugs pulling 'tow-boats' containing horses, carriages and cars between Portsmouth and the George Street slipway in Ryde, moving later to Fishbourne. However, there were long delays in manoeuvring and loading the boats and in 1927 the first purpose-built car ferry, the 136 ton double-ended *Fishbourne,* entered service from the slipway at Point. In 1961, the terminal moved to a larger slipway further inside the Camber docks. Subsequent increases in the size of vessels eventually led to the conversion of the former collier dock at the nearby power station to provide the modern terminal at Gunwharf Road.

Now there is a modern fleet of five car ferries, four of the single-end-loading *St Catherine* type, and the newer *St Clare,* which returned to the double-ended design.

The paddle steamer *Whippingham*, built in 1930 for the Southern Railway, served on the Portsmouth to Ryde route until the early 1960s. (Stephen Cribb)

Brading was one of three diesel ferries built after the Second World War for the Portsmouth to Ryde service, and is seen here in Sealink colours arriving at Ryde pierhead.

St Catherine off the Point. (Author)

Our Lady Patricia leaving harbour. (Author)

She dwarfs the original vessels though, and carries 204 cars compared to the *Fishbourne's* sixteen.

Vessels in Service

Name	Entered Service	Cars	Passengers	Tonnage	Speed knots
St Catherine	1983	142	771	2036	12½
St Helen	1983	142	771	2983	12½
St Cecilia	1987	142	771	2968	12½
St Faith	1990	142	771	3009	12½
St Clare	2001	204	878	5359	13
Our Lady Patricia	1986		395	312	29
Our Lady Pamela	1986		395	312	29
Fastcat Shanklin	2000★		361	478	34
Fastcat Ryde	2000★		361	478	34

★ Built in 1996

CROSS-CHANNEL FERRIES

Portsmouth is now a leading port for cross-Channel ferries, the volume of traffic being exceeded only by Dover. The success of this development was due to successful exploitation of the growth in Channel crossings that has occurred since the 1960s, when Southampton was a base for such operations. With new motorway connections, quicker access to the Channel, and the building of the Ferryport at the eastern end of Fountain Lake, Portsmouth was able to wrest this trade from Southampton. The ferries themselves have grown in size and now the largest of them is bigger than many of the ocean liners which used Southampton in the heyday of ocean travel. *Pride of Bilbao* is bigger in gross tonnage than, for example, the Cunard Line's *Mauretania* of 1939. As they have grown in size, the large ferries have offered an increasing variety of on-board facilities including cinemas, shops, restaurants, bars, live entertainment, dancing, children's playrooms, sundecks, and on some, conference rooms, swimming pools and health suites. The main accommodation includes observation lounges and cabins for overnight travel. Smaller new fast ferries joined several of the services, carrying passengers and cars but not lorries. Travelling at speeds of up to 40 knots they nearly halved the crossing times to Cherbourg and Caen.

By 2004 P&O Ferries was operating to the French ports of Le Havre, Cherbourg and Caen, and to Bilbao in Spain. Whilst daytime crossing times to France were around five hours, or three hours on the fast craft, the Bilbao route takes thirty-five hours on the outward journey and twenty-nine hours on the return journey. Brittany Ferries were running to St Malo, a nine hour daytime crossing, and to Cherbourg and Caen. Overnight crossings are longer than daytime ones, allowing more time for sleep. A third operator, Condor Ferries ran to the Channel Isles (Jersey and Guernsey), and for freight, to St Malo. Condor's ships fly the flag of Bahamas and, like Wightlink, the company is owned by the Royal Bank of Scotland.

In September 2004 P&O announced that it was withdrawing from all of its Western Channel crossings, all of which operated from Portsmouth, dealing a body blow to the port. Only the Bilbao route was to be retained. The company blamed a decline in business caused by the abolition of duty-free sales, the increased taxes on French cigarettes, the rise in travel on low-cost airlines, and competition from the French government-subsidized Brittany Ferries. As a result, the two fast ferries (*Caen Express* and *Cherbourg Express*) and *Pride of Cherbourg* were withdrawn. A deal for Brittany Ferries to charter *Pride of Le Havre* and *Pride of Portsmouth* on the Le Havre route fell through. Meanwhile, Brittany Ferries announced the introduction of a fast ferry service to Caen and Cherbourg with their new *Normandie Express*.

Vessels in Service (2005)

Name	Built	Cars	Freight Vehicles	Passengers	Tonnage
P&O Ferries					
Pride of Bilbao	1986	600	65	2,500	37,583
Pride of Le Havre	1989	575	110	1,600	33,336
Pride of Portsmouth	1990	575	110	1,600	33,336
Brittany Ferries					
Barfleur	1992	590		1,212	20,133
Mont St Michel	2002	884		2,200	34,000
Normandie	1992	600	84	2,123	27,541
Normandie Express	2005	267		900	6,581
Pont Aven	2004	650	20	2,400	41,700
Val de Loire	1993	580	73	2,140	31,788
Condor Ferries					
Commodore Clipper	1999	279	92	500	13,466
Commodore Goodwill	1996			12	11,166

Routes (in 2005)

Bilbao: *Pride of Bilbao.*
Caen: *Mont St Michel, Normandie, Normandie Express.*
Cherbourg: *Normandie Express, Barfleur, Val de Loire.*
Le Havre: *Pride of Le Havre, Pride of Portsmouth.*
St Malo: *Val de Loire, Commodore Goodwill,* plus *Pont Aven* (Winter only).
Guernsey and Jersey: *Commodore Clipper, Commodore Goodwill.*

Normandie leaving the harbour. (Author)

Pride of Bilbao entering harbour with *Spirit of Gosport* in the foreground. (Author)

PADDLE STEAMER WAVERLEY

Although the last paddle steamer to sail regularly from Portsmouth, *Ryde*, was withdrawn in 1969 it is still possible to see the world's last sea-going paddle steamer, *Waverley,* when she visits the port for a period of about two weeks each year as part of her Round Britain cruising programme. Fully restored and painted in her original London & North Eastern Railway colours she makes an exciting sight as she enters and leaves the harbour under steam, calling at the Railway Pier at Portsmouth Harbour Station where *Ryde* and her sisters were once based.

Waverley was built for service on the Clyde by A&J Inglis at Glasgow and completed in 1947. Designed on pre-war paddle steamer lines, she was one of the last traditional paddle steamers to be built. She was coal-fired though was converted to burn oil in 1956. Her original colour scheme lasted only one season, for in 1948 the railways were nationalised and *Waverley's* funnels were repainted in the buff (pale yellow) with black tops colours of the Caledonian Steam Packet Co. For twenty-seven seasons she operated on the Clyde and surrounding area as both an excursion vessel and on regular local ferry services. In 1974 she was sold for a nominal £1 to the Paddle Steamer Preservation Society, thus saving her from the shipbreakers. Rather than becoming a static exhibit, she was refitted for the Waverley Steam Navigation Company, a limited company formed by the enthusiasts who had saved her, and in 1975 she re-entered service on the Clyde.

In 1981 she was fitted with a new boiler and embarked on her first season of Round Britain cruising, with the peak summer weeks spent back on the Clyde. This has extended her season considerably and has helped make her operation viable. In her winter 1990–1991 refit the paddle wheels were replaced and she continues to be maintained in excellent condition. Her splendid 66in-stroke triple-expansion engines can be viewed in operation by passengers on the main deck between the lounge and the restaurant.

Waverley leaving Portsmouth, September 2003. (Author)

Waverley entering Portsmouth Harbour. (Author)

Facts and Figures

Gross tonnage: 693 Length: 239.6ft/ 73m Beam: 30.2ft/ 17.45m Draught: 6.5ft/ 1.98m
Propulsion: Triple expansion diagonal steam engine, oil-fired, 2,100 IHP. Speed: 18.5
   knots
Passengers: 1,350
Launched: 2 October 1946 Completed: June 1947

THE PORTSMOUTH FLOTILLA

In 2002 the Royal Navy was reorganized into three flotillas, corresponding to the three home bases of Portsmouth, Devonport and Faslane. Details are given here of the classes included in the Portsmouth Flotilla. A complete list of Royal Navy ships is given on pages 145-148 together with their pennant numbers, builders and dates of completion. From time to time the Devonport and Faslane ships will be seen at Portsmouth.

AIRCRAFT CARRIERS

Invincible Class

Invincible, Illustrious and *Ark Royal* are the Navy's largest surface warships. At any time one is normally in full commission, a second is in reduced readiness, in refit or working up, whilst the third is in reserve. When ordered they were known as through-deck cruisers to circumvent the political decision to axe aircraft carriers in the 1970s. In fact they were originally designed as anti-submarine helicopter carriers and were equipped with Sea Dart ship-to air missiles. The development of the Sea Harrier vertical take-off and landing jet meant that they could become more versatile replacements for the Navy's fleet of larger fixed-wing aircraft carriers. The first of the class, *Invincible,* had been in service for nearly two years when the Falklands War erupted in April 1982. She was part of the task force led by *Hermes* which recaptured the islands. *Hermes* was the last of the previous generation of aircraft carriers, and was replaced by *Illustrious* which entered service only a week after the recapture of the Falklands and was immediately deployed to the South Atlantic. Ironically it had been announced just prior to the conflict that *Invincible* been sold to the Royal Australian Navy, a decision that was speedily reversed in the light of public outcry as the value of the ship became apparent. The third ship was originally to have been named *Indomitable* but was given the Navy's most famous carrier name, *Ark Royal,* whilst still under construction, the previous ship of the name having been scrapped

Invincible leaving Portsmouth. (Mark Teadham)

in 1980. *Illustrious* is also a famous carrier name, whilst *Invincible* was a battlecruiser sunk at Jutland: both these names were previously held by ships of the line.

The twelve degree angled 'ski-ramp' at the forward end of the flight deck allows the Harriers to take off more heavily laden, and the ships do not need the launching catapults or arrestor wires of previous generations of carriers. Now the class can be used for anti-submarine or amphibious operations, or in support of ground forces, using a mix of aircraft (Harriers or helicopters of a variety of types) to suit the circumstances. The Sea Harriers are being phased out and replaced by the RAF's slower ground attack versions of the Harrier, the GR7 and GR9 fitted with Sidewinder air-to-air missiles, primarily for self defence. This will reduce the air defence capability of the fleet until the proposed Joint Strike Fighter enters service in 2012. For close-in protection against anti-ship missiles, aircraft or surface vessels the ships are fitted with the Goalkeeper System in forward, starboard midships and aft positions. This system uses a seven barreled 30mm gun, firing at a rate of 4,200 rounds a minute, with a range of 1,500m. The *Invincible* Class can also serve as command ships for naval task groups. *Illustrious* served in the command ship and helicopter carrier role in 2002 in support of the operations in Afganistan, and *Ark Royal* served in this capacity in the second Gulf War in 2003. The class will operate until the two new, much larger, aircraft carriers (*Queen Elizabeth* and *Prince of Wales*) are commissioned in the next decade.

Facts and Figures

Displacement: 22,000 tonnes Length: 209.1m Beam: 33.5m Draught: 7m
Propulsion: four Rolls-Royce Olympus gas turbines, 72mw, 2 shafts. Speed: 28 knots
Armament: 24 aircraft, 2 x 20mmm guns, 3 Goalkeeper anti-aircraft/anti-missile systems.
Complement: 685 plus 386 aircrew. Military lift: up to 600 troops.

The Type 42 destroyer HMS *Southampton*. (Dave Page Collection)

DESTROYERS

Type 42

This class was introduced in 1975 to provide air defence to the fleet, based on the Sea Dart missile system and, later, the Phalanx Close-In Weapon System. The Sea Dart has a range of 20 nautical miles up to 60,000 feet, at a speed faster than Mach 2. The Phalanx 20mm rotary cannon can fire 3000 rounds per minute and has a range of 1,500m. As well as anti-aircraft and anti-missile roles the ships are equipped for surface and anti-submarine warfare through their armament of missiles, guns and torpedoes. They are powered by two dual sets of gas turbines, one pair for cruising and a further pair for maximum speed. The last four ships of the class (known as Batch 3) – *Edinburgh*, *Gloucester*, *Manchester* and *York* – are bigger in length and beam to give improved seakeeping and accommodation, and are distinguishable by their longer forecastle. The Type 42's were heavily involved in the Falklands War: *Sheffield* and *Coventry* were sunk and *Cardiff*, *Exeter* and *Glasgow* also saw action. The 'town' names of this class were previously held by cruisers, the size of the Type 42s having made them comparable with earlier generations of light cruiser. The *Birmingham* has been scrapped leaving a class of eleven ships, which will be replaced by the new Type 45 destroyers. Following the 2004 Defence Review *Newcastle* and *Glasgow* paid off in late 2004 and *Cardiff* was expected to follow in 2005.

Facts and Figures

Displacement: 4,820/*5,200* tonnes Length: 124.6/*141*m Beam: 14.3/*15.2*m Draught: 4.8/*4.5*m (Figures in italics refer to Batch 3)

Propulsion: two Tyne gas turbines, 8mw (cruising), and two Olympus gas turbines, 36 mw (full speed), 2 shafts. Speed: 30 knots.

Armament: Twin Sea Dart missile system, 2 x 20mm Phalanx systems, 1 x 114mm gun, 2 x 20mm guns, 6 x Stingray torpedo tubes, 1 Lynx helicopter armed with Stingray anti-submarine torpedoes and Sea Skua anti-ship missiles.

Complement: 287

Type 45

The Type 45 (*Daring* Class) destroyers are large warships displacing 7,350 tonnes with a new air defence missile system as their main armament. This Principal-Anti-Air-Missile-System (PAAMS) has been developed jointly with France and Italy, and accommodates the short range Aster 15 and the long range Aster 30 missiles, the latter having a speed in excess of Mach 4. Substantial growth margins have been incorporated into the ships' design which allow space and weight for future equipment. They will, for example, have the capacity to carry cruise missiles if future requirements deem this is to be necessary. The Type 45's are the largest general purpose warships to be built for the Navy since the Second World War and, along with the new aircraft carriers, will provide the backbone of the Royal Navy's air defences in the first half of the twenty-first century. Six vessels have been ordered. They are being built in modular fashion to be assembled by the prime contractor, BAE Systems, at their Yarrow, Scotstoun, yard on the Clyde. A further six ships were projected but this was reduced to two in the 2004 Defence Review.

Facts and Figures

Displacement: 7,350 tonnes Length: 152.4m Beam: 21.2m Draught: 5.0m

Propulsion: 2 x WR-21 gas turbines, 25 mw, plus 2 x electric motors, 25 mw, 2 shafts. Speed: 29 knots.

Range: 7,000 nautical miles at 18 knots.

Armament: 48 x Aster 15/30 missiles, 1 x 114mm and 2 x 30mm guns, 2 x Phalanx anti-air systems, 1 x Lynx or Merlin helicopter with Sea Skua missiles and Stingray torpedoes.

Complement: 190 (with space for 235). Plus up to 60 Royal Marines.

FRIGATES

Type 23 (Duke Class)

These frigates were designed for anti-submarine warfare in the North Atlantic during the Cold War period but do have extensive capability for anti-ship, air defence and shore bombardment. This more powerful weapon outfit resulted from the lessons of the Falklands War, in which destroyers and frigates were found to have poor self-defence capabilities and four ships were lost. The anti-submarine capability is provided by a towed sonar array and Stingray torpedoes launched from the ship and from its Lynx helicopter (which is being replaced on this class by the much larger Merlin helicopter). Four torpedo tubes are built into the sides of the hangar structure. As with the fixed Sea Wolf silos, this arrangement dramatically reduces the exposure of personnel on the upper deck in action by obviating the need to reload torpedo tubes or missile launchers. The Sea Wolf missiles provide air defence with a range of 10km. The Harpoon missiles are an anti-ship weapon, with a range of 130km and a cruising speed of Mach 0.9. The Sea Skua anti-ship missile is carried by the helicopter and has a range of 15km at a high subsonic speed. These are augmented by the 114mm gun for air and surface targets as well as shore bombardment, with a range of 22km and able to fire twenty-five rounds per minute. The Type 23s were the first ships in the Royal Navy to be designed as stealth vessels with the elimination of as much heat, noise and reflection as possible. Quiet running at slow speeds is possible, when searching for submarines, by using the direct drive electric propulsion motors powered by four diesel generators. Two Rolls-Royce Spey gas turbines are the main propulsion for full speed operation. The geometry of the hull and superstructure is designed to prevent radar beams being reflected back to incoming missiles. The sixteen ships of the class are named, somewhat anachronistically, after dukes. The names are nevertheless rather ambiguous, leading to the criticism that one, *St Albans*, has been named after a shopping centre. Under the 2004 Defence Review it was announced that *Norfolk, Marlborough* and *Grafton* would be withdrawn by March 2006 despite being modern ships. *Marlborough* was due to pay off in June 2005 after the Spithead Review.

Facts and Figures

Displacement: 4,900 tonnes Length: 133m Beam: 16.1m Draught: 5m
Propulsion: Combined diesel-electric and gas turbines – two Rolls-Royce Spey gas
    turbines, 25mw; four GEC-Alsthom Paxman Valenta diesels; plus two electric motors,
    3mw; 2 shafts. Speed: 28 knots.
Armament: 32 x Sea Wolf (silo missile launcher), 8 x Harpoon missile launchers,
    1 x 114mmm gun, 2 x 30mm guns, 4 x Stingray torpedo tubes, 1 Lynx or Merlin
    helicopter.
Complement: 185.

MINE COUNTERMEASURES VESSELS

Hunt Class

Designed by Vosper Thornycroft, who also built most of the class, the Hunts have non-magnetic glass reinforced plastic (GRP) hulls and an extra, low noise, diesel engine for use in slow speed operations. These characteristics allow them to operate safely in the area of magnetic and acoustic mines. They are able to conduct both minesweeping and minehunting operations and have seen service in the Falklands and the Gulf countering live mines. They destroy mines by sweeping them from astern with towed wire or influence sweeps (both magnetic and acoustic), or hunt them using sonar to detect the mines ahead of the ship. Swept mines are destroyed by gunfire or exploded by the influence sweep. Mines detected by sonar are destroyed by explosive charges laid either by

The Hunt-class mine countermeasures ship *Quorn* entering Portsmouth Harbour. (Mark Teadham)

a diver or by the ship's two unmanned submersibles, looking like miniature submarines, which are remotely controlled from the ship. Hunt names were first used on First World War minesweepers, and then on escort destroyers in the Second World War.

Two of the class were sold to Greece in 2000. The remaining ships are based at Portsmouth and Faslane. Under the 2004 Defence Review it was announced that *Brecon*, *Dulverton* and *Cottesmore* would pay off by April 2007. (These three ships constitute the Northern Ireland Squadron and their minesweeping gear has been replaced by two cranes serving Pacific rigid inflatable boats, which are used to intercept other vessels in counter-terrorism operations.)

Facts and Figures

Displacement: 750 tonnes Length: 60m Beam: 10.5m Draught: 2.2m
Propulsion: three diesel engines, 1.5mw, 2 shafts and bow thruster. Speed: 15 knots.
Armament: 1 x 30mm gun.
Complement: 45.

Sandown Class

This class of single-role minehunters was designed as a cheaper alternative to the Hunts. They have GRP hulls and, as well as the main diesel propulsion, have two electric motors for quiet slow running when minehunting. Instead of conventional propellers, each ship has two Voith Scheider propulsors: the propulsor consists of five blades hanging down from a rotating carousel. By altering the pitch of the blades thrust can be applied in any direction. Used in conjunction with the ship's two bow thrusters, the ship can move in any direction or keep an exact position regardless of wind and tide. In appearance they are rather ugly slab-sided craft.

The class took names of small coastal towns previously borne by First and Second World War minesweepers. *Cromer* is now a training ship for the Royal Naval College at Dartmouth, and the other ships are based at Portsmouth and Faslane. Ships of this class have been deployed on Gulf operations, and three ships were built for the Saudi Arabian Navy. In the 2004 Defence Review it was announced that *Inverness*, *Bridport* and *Sandown* would pay off by April 2005 despite being modern ships.

Facts and Figures

Displacement: 600 tonnes Length: 52.5m Beam: 10.9m Draught: 2.3m
Propulsion: three diesel engines, 1mw, and two 100kw electric motors, 2 shafts and twin
   bow thruster. Speed: 13 knots.
Armament: 1 x 30mm gun.
Complement: 34.

PATROL VESSELS

River Class

These three offshore patrol vessels were built by Vosper Thornycroft to its own account for leasing to the Royal Navy, for five years in the first instance. The contract includes the support and maintenance of the ships. Built to replace the Island class, they are used mainly for fishery protection duties and carry two Halmatic Pacific boarding and rescue boats. They also carry out regular surveillance patrols of the UK's offshore gas and oilfield installations. With a rotating crew system each vessel is expected to spend twice as many days at sea than the Island class vessels. *Mersey* was the last RN ship to be built at VT's Woolston shipyard before its shipbuilding activities relocated to Portsmouth Dockyard.

The Sandown-class minehunter *Inverness* entering Portsmouth Harbour. (Mark Teadham)

Facts and Figures

Displacement: 1,677 tonnes Length: 79.5m Beam: 13.6m Draught: 3.8m

Propulsion: two diesel engines, 4.1mw, one shaft plus 280 kw bow thruster. Speed: 16.5 knots (maximum 20 knots). Range: 5,500 nautical miles at 15 knots.

Armament: 1 x 20mm gun.

Complement: 30 plus Royal Marine boarding party (total accommodation 48).

Castle Class

The design of the Castle class incorporates a large flight deck which can operate helicopters as big as the Sea King, making the two ships very flexible in their operations. They embark a Royal Marine detachment and carry two Avon Sea Rider boarding and rescue boats. They are fitted with a sophisticated navigation and tracking system to locate and intercept other vessels. They also carry detergent spraying equipment for the dispersal of oil slicks. One ship is normally on long term patrol duties off the Falkland Islands, whilst the other forms part of the Fishery Protection Squadron together with the River class vessels. Both of the Castle class are to be replaced by a single vessel, *Clyde*, being built by VT – a modified version of the River class which will incorporate a helicopter flight deck.

Facts and Figures

Displacement: 1,427 tonnes Length: 81m Beam: 11.5m Draught: 3.6m

Propulsion: two diesel engines, 4.2mw, two shafts. Speed: 20 knots.

Armament: 1 x 30mm gun.

Complement: 45 plus 25 Royal Marines.

Endurance

The distinctive red hull of HMS *Endurance* allows easy recognition, especially from the air, in the ice of the Antarctic, the region in which she spends seven months of each year. Her duties include hydrographic survey work, the support of British Antarctic Survey scientists, and the support of British interests in Antarctic waters. As well as deep water survey she is equipped with two inshore survey motor boats which can operate independently from each other and from the ship. Much of the area is still being charted for the first time and the data gathered are processed by the Hydrographic Office at Taunton and drawn into charts that are used by mariners around the world. Her flight deck and hangar allow the operation of two Lynx helicopters. She is a Class One icebreaker, having been built in Norway as MV *Polar Circle* and was initially chartered as HMS *Polar Circle* in 1991. Purchased outright by the Navy in 1992, she was renamed *Endurance* after the ship she replaced and, originally, the ship used by Shackleton for his 1914 Antarctic expedition. She was designated to act as the Queen's yacht, providing a viewing platform as she proceeds through the lines at the 2005 Spithead Review.

The fast training boat HMS *Pursuer.* (Dave Page Collection)

Facts and Figures

Displacement: 5,500 tonnes Length: 91m Beam: 17.9m Draught: 6.6m
Propulsion: two diesel engines, 6mw, one shaft plus bow and stern thrusters. Speed: 14 knots
Aircraft: two helicopters.
Complement: 112 plus 14 Royal Marines.

Archer Class

These fast training boats are used to provide seagoing training for undergraduates of the fourteen University Royal Naval Units around the UK and are based in ports close to their respective universities. Each unit is commanded by a RN lieutenant who is responsible for fifty-one undergraduates who each join as RN Reservists for their time at university. Seagoing training is conducted over weekends and during the vacations in the *Archer* class patrol craft attached to each unit. Together these fourteen boats form the First Patrol Boat Squadron and are part of the Portsmouth Flotilla. Two further craft, *Dasher* and *Pursuer*, are based at Cyprus to patrol the waters around the Sovereign Base Area. The *Archer* class boats have GRP hulls and are not normally armed.

Facts and Figures

Displacement: 54 tonnes Length: 20.8m Beam: 5.8m Draught: 1.8m
Propulsion: two Perkins diesel engines (except *Raider* and *Tracker* which have two MTU V12 diesels).
Speed: 20 knots (*Raider* and *Tracker* 24 knots) Range: 550 nautical miles at 15 knots.
Complement: 5 (plus 12 undergraduates).

THE ROYAL FLEET AUXILIARY

The Royal Fleet Auxiliary supports the Royal Navy in its overseas operations such as in the Arabian Gulf, South Atlantic, Indian Ocean and the West Indies. The ships of the RFA are civilian-manned under Merchant Navy conditions. They operate away from the UK for extended periods and most do not have home base ports, but can be seen at Portsmouth from time to time, sometimes at the Forton Oil Jetty.

The core of the fleet is the tankers and storeships which are all equipped for replenishment of warships with fuel, ammunition, food and equipment whilst underway at sea. This is accomplished by the warship and RFA steaming along side-by-side and transferring fuel or stores by hoses and lines rigged between them. Newest of these ships are the two Wave-class fast tankers which have electric propulsion, are equipped with a helicopter platform aft and can support large task forces. They are supplemented by the three smaller Rover class which are used to replenish individual warships or small groups on deployment. The four Leaf-class tankers are used for the bulk freighting of fuel between Ministry of Defence bases and are also equipped for replenishment at sea. The RFA tankers can carry some food and stores, but the dual-purpose *Fort George* and *Fort Victoria* combine the roles of fleet oilers and stores ships, having considerably more space for dry stores than the tankers. Two earlier ships, *Fort Austin* and *Fort Rosalie*, are stores ships which, like the other two Forts have a large helicopter platform and hangar and are able to operate four or five Sea King helicopters.

There are two specialist RFA ships: *Argus* is used for helicopter training and as a casualty-receiving ship, whilst *Diligence* is a repair ship which provides forward repair and maintenance to ships and submarines on overseas deployment. The RFA also operates the Knight-class landing ships which are being replaced by the much larger Bay class. All of the RFA fleet is listed on pages 145-148 with their A and L pennant numbers.

RFA *Blue Rover.* (Dave Page Collection)

Marine Services

A fleet of tugs, tenders, mooring vessels, armament carriers and other specialist vessels is operated by the Royal Maritime Auxiliary Service and private contractors for harbour and coastal work associated with naval operations around the UK. Most of the ships have black hulls and buff upperworks though may occasionally be painted in the contractor's colours. Tugs such as *Bustler, Powerful, Setter, Helen* and *Genevieve* are used for towage and berthing duties at Portsmouth, where the twin-hulled *Newhaven, Netley, Nutbourne,* and *Padstow* serve as tenders. *Moorhen* is a mooring vessel at the port, and the armament carrier *Kinterbury* was frequently seen until being withdrawn in late 2004.

Name	Penn No	Built	Tonnage	Length	Beam	Draught	Speed
Bustler	A225	1981	375	39	10	4	12
Genevieve	A150	1980	89	21.5	6.4	2.8	9
Helen	A198	1974	89	21.5	6.4	2.8	9
Kinterbury	A378	1981	1,393	70.6	11.9	4.6	14
Moorhen	Y32	1989	518	32	11	2	8
Netley	A282	2001	77	18.3	6.8	1.9	10
Newhaven	A280	2000	77	18.3	6.8	1.9	10
Nutbourne	A281	2000	77	18.3	6.8	1.9	10
Padstow	A286	2000	77	18.3	6.8	1.9	10
Powerful	A223	1985	375	39	10	4	12
Setter	A189	1969	151	28.6	7.4	3	10

RFA *Fort Grange* (since renamed *Fort Rosalie*). (Dave Page Collection)

RFA *Fort George*. (Dave Page Collection)

The harbour tug *Setter*, completed in 1969, is manned by the RMAS and based at Portsmouth. (Author)

The harbour tug *Powerful*, completed in 1985, and her sister ship *Bustler*, are the largest tugs at Portsmouth. (Author)

The armament carrier *Kinterbury* was built in 1981 for the transportation of armaments between bases, and occasionally is used in support of naval trials and exercises. She is seen here leaving Portsmouth. (Author)

INDEX OF ROYAL NAVY SHIPS
AND ROYAL FLEET AUXILIARIES

Pennant No.	Name	Class	Completed	Builder
Aircraft Carriers				
R05	*Invincible*	Invincible	1979	Vickers
R06	*Illustrious*	,,	1982	Swan Hunter
R07	*Ark Royal*	,,	1985	,,
Amphibious Warfare Ships				
L10	*Fearless*★★	Fearless	1965	Harland & Wolff
L11	*Intrepid*★★	,,	1967	John Brown
L12	*Ocean*	Ocean	1998	Kvaerner
L14	*Albion*	Albion	2003	BAE Systems
L15	*Bulwark*	,,	2004	,,
L3004	*Sir Bedivere*	Knight	1967	Hawthorn Leslie
L3005	*Sir Galahad*	,,	1987	Swan Hunter
L3006	*Largs Bay*	Bay	2005	,,
L3007	*Lyme Bay*★	,,		,,
L3008	*Mounts Bay*★	,,		,,
L3009	*Cardigan Bay*★	,,		,,
L3027	*Sir Geraint*★★	Knight	1967	Stephen
L3036	*Sir Percivale*★★	,,	1968	Hawthorn Leslie
L3505	*Sir Tristram*	,,	1967	,,
Destroyers				
D23	*Bristol*★★★	Type 82	1972	Swan Hunter
D32	*Daring*★	Type 45		BAE Systems
D33	*Dauntless*★	,,		,,
D34	*Diamond*★	,,		,,
D35	*Dragon*★	,,		,,
D36	*Defender*★	,,		,,
D37	*Duncan*★	,,		,,
D87	*Newcastle*★★	Type 42	1978	Swan Hunter

D88	Glasgow★★	,,	1978	,,
D89	Exeter	,,	1980	,,
D90	Southampton	,,	1981	Vosper Thornycroft
D91	Nottingham	,,	1982	,,
D92	Liverpool	,,	1982	Cammell Laird
D95	Manchester	,,	1983	Vickers
D96	Gloucester	,,	1984	Vosper Thornycroft
D97	Edinburgh	,,	1985	Cammell Laird
D98	York	,,	1984	Swan Hunter
D108	Cardiff	,,	1979	Vickers

Frigates

F78	Kent	Type 23	2000	Yarrow
F79	Portland	,,	2000	,,
F80	Grafton	,,	1996	,,
F81	Sutherland	,,	1997	,,
F82	Somerset	,,	1996	,,
F83	St Albans	,,	2001	,,
F85	Cumberland	Type 22	1988	,,
F86	Campbeltown	,,	1988	Cammell Laird
F87	Chatham	,,	1989	Swan Hunter
F99	Cornwall	,,	1987	Yarrow
F229	Lancaster	Type 23	1991	,,
F230	Norfolk★★	,,	1989	,,
F231	Argyll	,,	1991	,,
F233	Marlborough	,,	1991	Swan Hunter
F234	Iron Duke	,,	1992	Yarrow
F235	Monmouth	,,	1993	,,
F236	Montrose	,,	1993	,,
F237	Westminster	,,	1993	Swan Hunter
F238	Northumberland	,,	1994	,,
F239	Richmond	,,	1994	,,

Submarines

S20	Astute★	Astute		BAE Systems
S21	Ambush★	,,		,,
S22	Artful★	,,		,,
S28	Vanguard	Vanguard	1992	VSEL
S29	Victorious	,,	1994	,,
S30	Vigilant	,,	1997	,,
S31	Vengeance	,,	1999	,,
S91	Trenchant	Trafalgar	1989	Vickers
S92	Talent	,,	1990	,,
S93	Triumph	,,	1991	,,
S104	Sceptre	Swiftsure	1978	,,
S105	Spartan	,,	1979	,,
S107	Trafalgar	Trafalgar	1983	,,
S108	Sovereign	Swiftsure	1974	,,
S109	Superb	,,	1976	,,
S110	Turbulent	Trafalgar	1984	,,
S117	Tireless	,,	1985	,,
S118	Torbay	,,	1986	,,

Mine Countermeasures Vessels

M29	Brecon	Hunt	1980	Vosper Thornycroft
M30	Ledbury	,,	1981	,,
M31	Cattistock	,,	1982	,,
M32	Cottesmore	,,	1983	Yarrow
M33	Brocklesby	,,	1983	Vosper Thornycroft
M34	Middleton	,,	1984	Yarrow
M35	Dulverton	,,	1983	Vosper Thornycroft
M37	Chiddingfold	,,	1984	,,
M38	Atherstone	,,	1987	,,
M39	Hurworth	,,	1985	,,
M41	Quorn	,,	1989	,,
M101	Sandown★★	Sandown	1989	,,
M102	Inverness★★	,,	1991	,,
M103	Cromer★★★	,,	1991	,,
M104	Walney	,,	1992	,,
M105	Bridport★★	,,	1993	,,
M106	Penzance	,,	1998	,,
M107	Pembroke	,,	1998	,,
M108	Grimsby	,,	1999	,,
M109	Bangor	,,	2000	,,
M110	Ramsey	,,	2000	,,
M111	Blyth	..	2001	,,
M112	Shoreham	,,	2001	,,

Patrol Vessels

P163	Express	Archer	1988	Vosper Thornycroft
P164	Explorer	,,	1985	Watercraft
P165	Example	,,	1985	,,
P167	Exploit	,,	1988	Vosper Thornycroft
P258	Leeds Castle	Castle	1981	Hall Russell
P264	Archer	Archer	1985	Watercraft
P265	Dumbarton Castle	Castle	1982	Hall Russell
P270	Biter	Archer	1985	Watercraft
P272	Smiter	,,	1986	,,
P273	Pursuer	,,	1988	Vosper Thornycroft
P274	Tracker	,,	1998	Ailsa Troon
P275	Raider	,,	1998	,,
P279	Blazer	Archer	1988	Vosper Thornycroft
P280	Dasher	,,	1988	,,
P281	Tyne	River	2002	,,
P282	Severn	,,	2003	,,
P283	Mersey	,,	2003	,,
P284	Scimitar	Scimitar	1988	Halmatic
P285	Sabre	'	1988	'
P291	Puncher	Archer	1988	Vosper Thornycroft
P292	Charger	,,	1988	,,
P293	Ranger	,,	1988	,,
P294	Trumpeter	,,	1988	,,

Survey Ships

H86	*Gleaner*	Gleaner	1983	Emsworth
H87	*Echo*	Echo	2002	Appledore
H88	*Enterprise*	Echo	2003	,,
H130	*Roebuck*	Roebuck	1986	Brooke Marine
H131	*Scott*	Scott	1997	Appledore

Royal Fleet Auxiliaries and Ice Patrol Ship

A81	*Brambleleaf*	Leaf	1980	Cammell Laird
A109	*Bayleaf*	,,	1982	Cammell Laird
A110	*Orangeleaf*	,,	1982	,,
A111	*Oakleaf*	Oakleaf	1981	Uddevalla
A132	*Diligence*	Diligence	1981	Oesundsvarvet
A134	*Rame Head*★★	Head	1945	Burrard Dry Dock
A135	*Argus*	Argus	1981	Cantieri Navali Breda
A171	*Endurance*	Endurance	1990	Ulstein–Hatlo
A269	*Grey Rover*	Rover	1970	Swan Hunter
A271	*Gold Rover*	,,	1974	,,
A273	*Black Rover*	,,	1974	,,
A385	*Fort Rosalie*	Fort I	1978	Scott Lithgow
A386	*Fort Austin*	,,	1979	,,
A387	*Fort Victoria*	Fort II	1992	Harland & Wolff
A388	*Fort George*	,,	1993	Swan Hunter
A389	*Wave Knight*	Wave	2002	BAE Systems
A390	*Wave Ruler*	,,	2002	,,

★ Under construction
★★ Paid off for disposal
★★★ In commission as static training ship

HMS *Invincible*, close up. (Author)

BUILDINGS AND DOCKS AT PORTSMOUTH DOCKYARD

Dry Docks and Locks

Dock No.	Opened	Closed	Notes
1	1801	1984	Now holds monitor *M33*
2	1802	1922	Now holds HMS *Victory*
3	1803	1982	Now holds *Mary Rose*
4	1772	1983	
5	1698	1983	Lengthened in 1850
6	1700	1984	Lengthened in 1908
7	1849	1984	Filled in 1989
8	1853		
9	1875		
10	1858	1989	Filled in.
11	1865		
12	1876		
13	1876	2001	Filled in 2002 for VT Group
14	1896		Lengthened in 1914
15	1896		Lengthened in 1907
Lock A	1875		
Lock B	1875		
Lock C	1913		
Lock D	1914		

Basins and Camber

Facility	Opened	Notes
No.1 Basin	1698	Enlarged 1769
Camber	1785	
No.2 Basin	1848	
No.3 Basin	1876	Originally three interconnected basins

Buildings

Map Ref	Building	Date	Map Ref	Building	Date
16	Porters' Lodge	1708	32	St Anne's Church	1785
			33	Offices	1786
17	Main (Victory) Gate	1711	34	Short Row	1787
18	Long Row	1717	35	Admiralty House	1787
19	Old Navy Academy	1729	36	Blacksmiths' Shop	1791
20	North Storehouse (No.11 Store)★	1763	37	Blockmills	1802
21	Hatchelling House	1770	38	Naval Archt. School	1816
22	Great Ropehouse	1770	39	Yard Water Tank	1843
			40	No.6 Boathouse	1845
23	Hemp Tarring House (Boiler Shop)	1771	41	Steam Factory	1849
24	East Sea Store (No.15 Store)	1771			
25	West Hemp House (No.16 Store)	1771	42	Pattern Shop and Foundry	1854
26	Middle Storehouse (No.10 Store)	1776	43	Armour Plate Shop	1867
27	East Hemp House (No.17 Store)	1781	44	No.7 Boathouse	1875
28	South Storehouse (No.9 Store)	1782	45	No.5 Boathouse★★	1882
			46	Police Cells	1882
29	Storehouse (SE Building)	1782	47	Mould Loft Floor	1891
30	Storehouse (SW Building)	1782	48	Railway Shelter	1893
31	Storehouse (NW Building)	1782	49	Semaphore Tower	1926

★ Royal Naval Museum ★★ Mary Rose Museum

A view of the dockyard, 1904. In the foreground is the Middle Storehouse. (Portsmouth City Libraries)

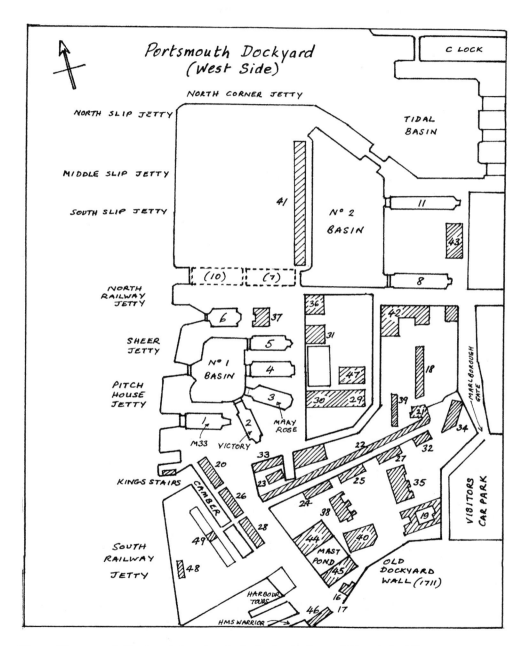

Plans of Portsmouth Dockyard showing docks, basins, jetties amd historic buildings.

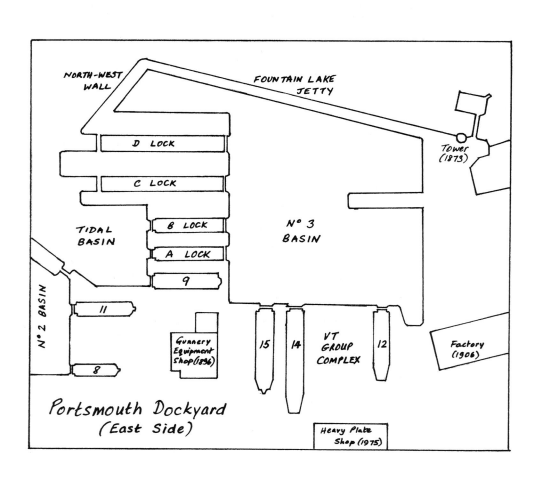

NORTH-WEST WALL

FOUNTAIN LAKE JETTY

Tower (1873)

D LOCK

C LOCK

B LOCK

A LOCK

9

N° 3 BASIN

TIDAL BASIN

N° 2 BASIN

11

8

Gunnery Equipment Shop (1896)

15

14

VT GROUP COMPLEX

12

Factory (1906)

Portsmouth Dockyard (East Side)

Heavy Plate Shop (1975)

TIMELINE FOR MARITIME PORTSMOUTH

284	Carausius appointed Count of the Saxon Shore, at Portchester, by the Romans to repel Saxon raiders.
501	Saxons seized land at Portsmouth.
1066	Harold's fleet assembled in the Solent but the expected invasion fleet was not sighted.
1114	King Henry I embarked from Portsmouth for Normandy (and subsequently in 1123, and probably 1133).
1174	King Henry II embarked from Portsmouth for Normandy.
1180	Jean de Gisors, a Norman merchant, founded a town in the area now known as Old Portsmouth.
1189	Richard the Lionheart landed at Portsmouth to become King of England.
1194	King Richard I granted Portsmouth its first charter.
1194	King Richard I ordered the building of a dock.
1212	King John ordered the enclosure of the dock and the building of storehouses.
1214	King John sailed for France in an unsuccessful attempt to re-establish lost territory.
1346	King Edward III sailed for Normandy and the Battle of Crecy.
1415	King Henry V sailed for France and the Battle of Agincourt.
1420	Earliest recorded ferry service from Portsmouth to Ryde, Isle of Wight.
1494	The Round Tower was reconstructed in stone.
1495	King Henry VII ordered the first dry dock to be built on the new dockyard site at Portsmouth.
1497	The first ship, the *Sweepstake*, was built in the dockyard.
1511	Completion of the *Mary Rose* at Portsmouth.
1538	Southsea Castle was built.
1545	French invasion attempt and the sinking of the *Mary Rose*.
1586	Sir Walter Raleigh imported potatoes and tobacco from Virginia at the Camber.
1588	Defeat of the Spanish Armada; included action off the Isle of Wight.
1623	Original dry dock filled in.
1649	*Parliamentarians abolished the monarchy (restored 1660).*
1651	New building slip laid down as part of a regeneration scheme including ropery and workshops.
1652	*Start of the First Dutch War (ended 1654).*
1658	Completion of new double dry dock.

1665	King Charles II authorized Sir Bernard de Gomme to proceed with fortifications in (Old) Portsmouth.
1665	*Start of the Second Dutch War (ended 1667).*
1672	*Start of the Third Dutch War (ended 1673).*
1677	King Charles II authorized Sir Bernard de Gomme to build the Gosport Lines (fortifications) including Forts Charles and James and the re-arming of Fort Blockhouse.
1689	*Start of war with France – War of the English Succession (ended 1697).*
1691	Work on two new wet docks and two dry docks commenced.
1698	Opening of the Great Basin (now No.1 Basin).
1702	*Start of war with France and Spain – War of the Spanish Succession (ended 1713).*
1718	*War with Spain (ended 1720).*
1733	The Royal Naval Academy opened as a college for naval officers.
1739	*War with Spain, called the War of Jenkins' Ear (also, later, with France). Peace came in 1749.*
1753	Opening of Haslar Hospital.
1756	*Start of the Seven Years War with France (ended 1763).*
1770	Opening of the Great Ropehouse.
1771	Completion of the Powder Magazine and camber basin at Priddy's Hard.
1773	Review of the fleet at Spithead by King George III.
1775	*Rebellion in the American colonies.*
1778	*War with France; Spain declared war against England in 1779, as did Holland in 1781.*
1783	*Peace with France, Spain, Holland and the United States of America.*
1787	Completion of Admiralty House, for Dockyard Commissioner.
1792	Francis Amos established a boat-building yard on the Fort Charles site, later Camper & Nicholsons.
1793	*War with France, the Revolutionary Wars (peace in 1802, but war recommenced in 1803).*
1797	The first steam engine was installed in the dockyard, to power a pump for draining dry docks.
1798	*Nelson's victory over the French at the Battle of the Nile.*
1801	*Nelson's victory over Russian, Danish and Swedish ships at the Battle of Copenhagen.*
1805	*Battle of Trafalgar.*
1812	*War with the United States of America.*
1815	*End of the French Revolutionary and Napoleonic Wars. Peace with the USA.*
1828	Royal Clarence Yard, victualling yard, opened at Gosport.
1835	Launch of the *Hermes*, the first steam-driven warship built by Portsmouth Dockyard.
1848	Launch of the *Leander*, the last sailing warship built at Portsmouth Dockyard.
1848	Opening of the Steam Basin (now No.2 Basin) by Queen Victoria.
1849	Opening of the Steam Factory.
1860	Palmerston ordered the construction of a ring of protective forts on Portsdown Hill and in the Solent.
1867	Plans for the Great Extension to the Dockyard were approved.
1871	Launch of the *Devastation*, the first iron-hulled battleship built at Portsmouth.
1871	Herbert Vosper established his ship repair (and, later, ship building company) in the Camber.
1876	Opening of the Great Extension. Launch of the battleship *Inflexible*.
1891	HMS *Excellent*, gunnery school, commissioned on Whale Island.
1905	Commissioning of HMS *Dolphin*, the Navy's first submarine base.
1906	Launch of the *Dreadnought*, the first steam-turbine powered battleship.
1914	*Start of the Great War (ended 1918).*
1922	HMS *Victory* was moved into dry dock for restoration and display (opened to public 1928).
1939	*Start of the Second World War (ended 1945).*

1944 Embarkation in Portsmouth Harbour and Stokes Bay for the D-Day landings in Normandy.

1967 Launch of the frigate *Andromeda*, the last warship built by the Royal Dockyard.

1975 Opening of the continental Ferry Port.

1981 The submarine *Alliance* was opened to the public at the Royal Naval Submarine Museum.

1982 Raising of the *Mary Rose*.

1984 Royal Dockyard renamed Portsmouth Naval Base, and Fleet Maintenance and Repair Organisation took over refitting and repairs.

1987 HMS *Warrior* returned to Portsmouth.

1989 Closure of the armament depot at Priddy's Hard.

1985 Closure of the gunnery school on Whale Island.

1994 The last operational submarine left HMS *Dolphin*, and the base was decommissioned in 1998.

1998 Portsmouth's first International Festival of the Sea.

2004 Shipbuilding resumed in the dockyard at Vosper Thornycroft's new facility.

HMS *Iron Duke*. (Author)

The Royal Yacht *Victoria and Albert* with Queen Victoria aboard, at Portsmouth in 1906. To the left is the battleship *Renown* whilst on the right can be seen HMS *Victory*. (Portsmouth City Libraries)

The launch of the battleship *Queen Elizabeth* in 1913. (Portsmouth City Libraries)

BIBLIOGRAPHY

Archibald, E., (1972) *The Wooden Fighting Ship*, Poole: Blandford.

Bardell, M. (2001) *Portsmouth, History and Guide*, Stroud: Tempus.

Bradford, E. (1982) *The Story of the Mary Rose*, London: Hamish Hamilton.

Brown, D., (1987) *The Royal Navy and the Falklands War*, London: Lee Cooper.

Brown, D.K., (1997) *Warrior to Dreadnought*, London: Chatham.

Brown, D.K., (1999) *The Grand Fleet*, London: Chatham.

Burton, L. (ed, 1986) *Attentive to Our Duty*, Gosport: Gosport Society.

Coad, J., (1983) *Historic Architecture of the Royal Navy*, London: Gollancz.

Dawson, C., (1972) *A Quest for Speed at Sea*, London: Hutchinson.

Defence Procurement Agency, (2003) *The Royal Navy Handbook*, London: Conway.

Dixon, C., (1987) *Ships of the Victorian Navy*, Shedfield: Ashford.

Evans, D., (2004) *Building the Steam Navy*, London: Conway.

Grundy, N., (1996) 'W L Wyllie, the Portsmouth Years', *Portsmouth Papers*, No. 68.

Hall, K., (2001) *HMS Dolphin, Gosport's Submarine Base*, Stroud: Tempus.

Ireland, B., (2000) *Naval Warfare in the Age of Sail*, London: HarperCollins.

Jones, J, (1993) *Historic Warships*, London: McFarland.

Lambert, A., (1987) *Warrior, Restoring the World's First Ironclad*, London: Conway.

Lipscomb, F., (1967) *Heritage of Sea Power*, London: Hutchinson.

MacDougall, P., (1982) *Royal Dockyards*, Vermont: David and Charles.

McGowan, A, (1999) *HMS Victory, Her Construction, Career, and Restoration*, London: Chatham.

McKendrick, J. *et al*, (1997) *Waverley, the Golden Jubilee*, Glasgow: Waverley Excursions.

National Maritime Museum, *Twentieth Century Warships – Service Histories: HMS Alliance*, Greenwich.

Patterson, B., (1989) *Giv'er a Cheer Boys: The Great Docks of Portsmouth Dockyard*, Portsmouth: Portsmouth Royal Dockyard Historical Society.

Riley, R., (1985) 'The Evolution of the Docks and Industrial Buildings in Portsmouth Royal Dockyard 1698 – 1914', *Portsmouth Papers*, No. 44.

Sadden, J., (2001) *Portsmouth, Heritage of the Realm*, Chichester: Phillimore.

Thomas, J., (1984) 'The Seaborn Trade of Portsmouth 1650 – 1800', *Portsmouth Papers*, No. 40.

Thomas, R. and Patterson, B., (1998) *Dreadnoughts in Camera*, Stroud: Sutton Publishing.

Warlow, B., (2000) *Shore Establishments of the Royal Navy*, Liskeard: Maritime Books.

Wells, J., (1980) *Whaley, the Story of HMS Excellent*, Portsmouth: HMS Excellent.

White, L., (1989) *The Story of Gosport*, Southampton: Ensign.

Williams, G., (1979) 'The Western Defences of Portsmouth Harbour 1400 – 1800', *Portsmouth Papers*, No.30.

Winton, J., (1989) *The Naval Heritage of Portsmouth*, Southampton: Ensign.

Wright, M., (2001) *It's Shorter by Water, the Gosport Ferry 1875-2001*, Michael Wright.

Websites

Preserved Ships

Portmouth Historic Dockyard – Mary Rose	www.flagship.org.uk/mary_rose
The News On-line Mary Rose Dossier	www.thenewscentre.co.uk/rose/disaster
BBC History – The Mary Rose	www.bbc.co.uk/history/mary_rose
HMS Warrior	www.hmswarrior.org
HMS Victory	www.hms-victory.com
HMS Bristol	www.southernseacadets.rg/bristolhistfile
Royal Naval Submarine Museum	www.rnsubmus.co.uk
Biber 105	www.fleet-support.co.uk/pr_biber
MTB 102	www.mtb102.com
Steam Pinnace 199	www.royalnavalmuseum.org/pinnace

News Stories – Royal Navy

Navy News	www.navynews.co.uk
Defence Procurement Agency	www.mod.uk/dpa
Fleet Support Limited	www.fleet-support.co.uk
Royal Navy	www.royal-navy.mod.uk

Facilities and Buildings

HMS Hornet	www.inadee.btinternet.co.uk/hhistory
Royal Dockyard	www.flagship.org.uk
Royal Naval Museum	www.royalnavalmuseum.org
The Porter's Garden	www.hants.org.uk/portersgarden
Spinnaker Tower	www.portsmouthand.co.uk/home/tower

Local History

Portsmouth History	www.portsmouthand.co.uk/history

Ferries

Brittany Ferries	www.brittany-ferries.co.uk
P&O Ferries	www.poferries.com
Portsmouth Continental Ferry Port	www.portsmouth-port.co.uk
Wightlink	www.wightlink.co.uk

Shipbuilding

Camper & Nicholsons	www.cnmarinas.com/history
Type 45 Destroyers	www.mod.uk/business/type45
Vosper Thornycroft (VT Shipbuilding)	www.vosperthornycroft.co.uk/shipbuilding

INDEX

If you are interested in purchasing other books published by Tempus, or in case you have difficulty finding any Tempus books in your local bookshop, you can also place orders directly through our website

www.tempus-publishing.com